-GUIDE FLIES-

~GUIDE FLIES~

How to Tie and Fish the KILLER FLIES
from AMERICA'S GREATEST Guides and Fly Shops

DAVID KLAUSMEYER

The Countryman Press

Woodstock, Vermont

Library of Congress Cataloging-in-Publication Data
Klausmeyer, David, 1958–
    Guide flies : how to tie and fish the killer flies from America's greatest guides and fly shops / David Klausmeyer.—1st ed.
        p. cm.
    ISBN 0-88150-582-X
        1. Fly tying—United States. 2. Flies, Artificial—United States. 3. Fishing guides—United States—Interviews. I. Title.

    SH451.K5298 2003
    688.7'9124—dc21

                                                                            2003055359

Cover and interior design by Carol Jessop, Black Trout Design
Cover and interior photographs by David Klausmeyer

Published by The Countryman Press, P.O. Box 748, Woodstock, VT 05091
Distributed by W. W. Norton & Company, Inc., 500 Fifth Avenue, New York NY 10110

Printed in Spain by Artes Graficas Toledo

10 9 8 7 6 5 4 3 2 1

~CONTENTS~

INTRODUCTION
working with a good guide

A guide is worth his (or her) weight in gold if he consistently puts you into fish.

I know some anglers wouldn't think of embarking on a fishing trip without hiring a guide. They prefer taking the fast track to the fish, and the advice of a good guide is the quickest way to finding fish when traveling to new waters. Some of these anglers also enjoy the company of a pleasant guide, especially if they're traveling alone; the guide just doesn't show the client to the fish, but fills the role of a companion for the day. The guide also takes care of many of the mundane tasks, such as hauling gear and perhaps preparing the meals. I know some lonesome doves who catch fish; they spend lots of time planning their trips, and research everything from where and when to fish, to which flies to bring. An experienced guide, however, can teach you the ins and outs of his local waters, and help you to find and catch more fish. But a guide can do so much more.

A really good guide will give you a greater appreciation for the local surroundings. He will point out interesting features and teach you about the local environment. He will also give you a sense of how the local people live and work. Maybe these are just my personal biases, but I like learning about these things when I travel. I could just string up my rod, cinch up my waders, put on blinders and fish my brains out, but that's a bore. I like to use fly fishing as a means to explore the world and meet new people. I've been fortunate to know guides who have helped me achieve these goals.

Writing about guides—and advising how to work with a guide—is a bit of a sticky subject. To start off, despite what the office-bound might think, guiding is a tough business with little glamour. Believe it or not, guides are not paid to fish. Many folks go into guiding because they love to fish and think it's a great way to be near the water. Yes, they get close to the water, but their job is to help others fish—at least that's what the best guides do.

I don't think anyone ever got rich in the guiding business. A guide might charge two, three, or four hundred dollars a day for his services (some saltwater guides who operate boats charge even more), and that might seem like a lot for a fishing trip, but it's not. Think about it: the guiding season probably doesn't last the entire year, and an independent guide must deduct his expenses—liability insurance, all equipment, advertising, fuel (for his vehicle and perhaps a boat), and food (if he provides a lunch and snacks). If he is honest with the government, a guide must pay income and social-security taxes on the money he earns. If he's trying to make guiding a full-time profession, he must pick up the tab for any health insurance costs. And, if the guide is really organized, he'll try to stash away a few bucks for the day when he can no longer row or pole a boat. Get the point? Guiding is a tough business not for the financial faint of heart.

Guiding is also physically demanding. While guides do enjoy many beautiful days on the water, they also spend hours in the pouring rain and getting eaten by mosquitoes. On balance, though, most guides love their jobs: the scenery, the independence, and the camaraderie of fellow anglers.

In addition to just pointing you to the fish and helping you appreciate the river and surrounding area, a good guide is also an instructor. If you're new to fly fishing, a guide can teach you the finer points of casting, rigging, knots, and fly selection. Open your mind, pay attention, and take advantage of the guide's knowledge.

Over the years, I've had the pleasure to fish with quite a few guides. There have been a couple of dogs in the bunch, but most have been very competent anglers—some have been really outstanding—who knew their waters and how to help others catch fish. They were a pleasure to be with, and I hope to spend time with them again. I've learned a lot from these guides and they've helped me to become a better angler.

I have also seen other anglers interact with guides. Some of these clients knew how to spoil the day almost from the beginning: they pretended to know more than the guide, they weren't interested in listening to the guide's advice, or they treated the guide like a common field hand rather than a professional. I've also seen other anglers sit back and let the guide take charge, and those clients usually had a really great day—even if they didn't catch fish. Let me share with you some of my observations about working with a guide. When you hire a guide it's your trip, but a professional guide knows how to show you a good time. Keep these things in mind and you'll increase the odds that you'll have a wonderful experience the next time you hire a guide.

I think the most important thing is to be honest with yourself—and the guide—about your skill level and abilities. Don't be afraid to admit that you're relatively new to fly fishing. Like all things in life, the journey of fly fishing requires taking the first steps. All guides tell me that they spend a lot of time just teaching some of their clients how to fish. A guide quickly learns that this goes with the job and they don't mind doing it. During the first hour or so of a trip, you're feeling out the guide ("can this guy really find fish?"), and the guide is also feeling you out ("can this guy really catch fish?"). Trust me: even the most experienced guides can get skunked by the fish, but it takes a guide only five minutes to see whether or not you can cast and do what it takes to catch fish.

A quality guide will be more than happy to spend time helping you improve your casting, showing you the proper way to tie a fly to the end of your leader, and teaching you how to spot and approach fish. It's your day, so make the most of it. Pick the guide's brain and absorb his knowledge. Be a sponge and ask questions—lots of questions.

An experienced angler should take the same approach to working with a guide. Remember that you're fishing on the guide's home waters and that he knows how to catch the local fish. You hired the guide to show you the ropes, so let him do his job. Again, pay attention and ask lots of questions. Your guide will be pleased to answer the more advanced queries that only a seasoned angler can ask, so take advantage of his knowledge.

An experienced angler should not bore the guide with stories about all of the other places that he's fished and about all of the big fish that he has caught. Swap stories over lunch, but don't start the day acting like a hotshot. Your guide will be much more impressed to see that you can cast and mend line well, and that you know how to set the hook and play fish. Lots of duffers brag about playing the best golf courses around the world, but no one is impressed to learn that they can't break a score of ninety. If you can cast a fly line, and know how to wade or handle yourself on a boat, your guide will be impressed and eager to help you catch fish.

Guides are great people who dedicate themselves to helping others have a good time. Frankly, I don't know how they do it; I don't have the patience. I'd give a client a shot at a nice fish, and if they'd blown it, I'd want to rip the rod out of their hands. "How could you do that?" I'd want to scream. "Do you know what you just did?" I admire guides who can relax and put up with the tomfoolery of people like me. A lot of guides and fly shops have shown patience by helping me put together this book. They supplied flies and answered my questions. I appreciate the time they took from their busy schedules. I've learned a lot, and I think you will, too.

This project is an outgrowth of another book I wrote for Countryman Press titled *Tying Contemporary Saltwater Flies.* While the focus of that volume is how to create patterns to catch striped bass, bluefish, bonefish, tarpon, permit, redfish, and a variety of other popular saltwater species, it also includes well over 100 patterns provided by guides from around the United States and abroad. They provided wonderful flies and information, and it seemed appropriate to expand on that theme and do a book containing freshwater patterns. And because this volume includes no actual illustrated tying steps (although there is a lot of tying advice), there is a lot more room to tell the full stories of the flies and the guides.

I'd like to thank all of the guides and fly-shop owners who submitted flies and offered their expertise.

David Klausmeyer

~FRESHWATER~
GUIDE FLIES

Sulfur Dun CDC Puff

tied by Tom Fink
Media, Pennsylvania

Hook: Regular dry-fly hook, sizes 18 and 16.
Thread: Yellow 8/0.
Tails: Ginger Microfibbetts.
Abdomen: Yellow turkey biot wrapped up the hook shank.
Thorax: Amber Superfine dubbing.
Wing: Two CDC feathers.

Cul de canard, also called CDC, is a high-floating feather from the rump of a duck. The theory is that these feathers are full of oil, and so resist absorbing water and remain afloat. Maybe these feathers do contain a high content of oil, but there seems to be more to it than this.

A few years, a great article appeared in *Fly Tyer* magazine that included photographs of CDC taken through a microscope. It turns out that the individual CDC fibers are full of tiny corkscrew-shaped hairs. The article argued, quite convincingly, that small air bubbles adhere to these hairs, and this is why the feather stays on the surface of the water.

Still not convinced? Consider this point: one of the first steps in the dyeing process is to degrease the feathers. This would remove all of the oil from the feathers, yet even dyed CDC floats like a cork.

Tom Fink, who guides out of The Sporting Gentleman, a fly shop in Media, Pennsylvania, fishes the Sulfur Dun CDC Puff from June through September during the afternoon and evening hatch. Tom likes to use lightweight tackle, and fishes this pattern with a 3-weight rod and 7X leader.

Mini-Max Parachute

tied by Ed Berg
San Pedro, California

Ed Berg isn't a guide, but he is a very talented fly tier. I met Ed at a fly-fishing show in Danbury, Connecticut, and was fascinated by his delicate parachute dry flies. I wrote about his patterns for *American Angler* magazine, and a lot of folks have told me that they found that article—and Ed's methods—to be very enlightening.

Ed ties these delicate parachutes very sparse. While this might seem difficult—many novice tiers always over-dress their flies—cutting back on the materials actually makes it easier to tie a dry fly.

"Twelve years ago, Northern California's catch-and-release lakes were proving to be a tough nut to crack by midsummer. The large resident trout had seen every fly out there, and they had all day to look over my offering before usually refusing it. Taking a good hard look at the natural mayfly sent me back to the bench to design a more realistic fly. The natural mayfly is an extremely delicate insect, far more delicate than my offerings. The design process was mainly one of subtraction. The more I took off, the better it worked."

While it would be difficult to describe all of the finer points of tying the Mini-Max Parachute without including a set of step-by-step tying instructions, here's one thing I think you'll find interesting. In order to create the wing, Ed folds a narrow piece of Z-Lon under the hook shank. He then ties off the Z-Lon with a couple of figure-eight wraps under the shank. This allows him to make the wing without adding bulk to the fly. It's a neat trick; give it a try.

Ed Berg likes to fish his delicate dun patterns fine and far off. He typically uses 3- or 4-weight rod and 15-foot-long, 6X or 7X leader.

Hook: Regular dry-fly hook, sizes 24 to 12.
Thread: Gudebrod 8/0 or 10/0.
Tails: Microfibbetts.
Body: Fine dry-fly dubbing.
Wing: White Z-Lon.
Hackle: Light dun.

Pink Coyote Hendrickson

tied by Scott Sickau
Boone, Iowa

Hook: Daiichi 1180, sizes 24 to 12.
Thread: White 8/0.
Tail: White hackle fibers.
Body: Pink urine-stained female coyote belly dubbing.
Wing: Natural mallard flank.
Hackle: White.

Hendricksons are found across North America, even in Iowa. The Pink Coyote Hendrickson is a simple imitation designed to match this important hatch. It can be tied in a wide variety of sizes, so match the material proportions—tail, wings, and hackle—to the hook.

Traditional Hendricksons were tied with the urine-stained underfur of a female fox. Scott Sickau's pattern uses the fur of a female coyote, a very inventive variation.

B.D.E. (Best Dry Ever)

tied by Ben Furimsky
Crested Butte, Colorado

Hook: Bent-shank scud hook, sizes 22 to 12.
Thread: Rust 8/0.
Tail and abdomen: Olive Gudebrod EZ-Dub.
Thorax: Peacock herl.
Hackle: Dun, spiral-wrapped over the thorax.
Wing: Dun polypropylene yarn.

Ben Furimsky is the son of Chuck Furimsky, the promoter of the International Fly Tying Symposium and a series of the largest fly-fishing consumer shows across the country. These shows are great because you'll be able to see the best fly tiers from around the world practicing their craft.

Ben's B.D.E. is a neat little mayfly dun that casts a realistic footprint on the water. To create the thorax, fray the end of a piece of EZ-Dub to create the tails of the fly. Add a drop of cement to the thorax and roll the body. Tie the extended body to the top of the hook and complete the fly.

The B.D.E. is a general dun imitation that can be tied in sizes to match most hatches.

Turck's Tarantula

tied by Guy Turck
Jackson, Wyoming

I first ran across the name "Guy Turck" while editing an article for *Fly Tyer* magazine about some of the best patterns used in the famous Jackson Hole One Fly competition. The One Fly is held every year to raise funds to protect the unique Snake River cutthroat trout. Jay Buchner, a guide who participates in the One Fly, collected about twenty patterns for that great article, and some of Guy Turck's flies were included.

A successful One Fly pattern must be superdurable. An angler can use only one fly—all day long. He may continue fishing if he looses his fly, but he may not score points for his team. And at the end of the day he receives bonus points if his fly is not falling apart. The demands of the One Fly have encouraged several local tiers to develop patterns to meet the demands of this unique event.

Turck's Tarantula is a great fly for fishing the Snake River, but it also catches fish across the country. When fishing Maine's West Branch of the Penobscot, guide Ian Cameron often turns to a Tarantula in the evening to catch that river's big landlocked salmon. Turck's Tarantula is a bushy floating pattern that can be used during a stonefly hatch, to imitate a grasshopper, or as an attractor; it's a fine alternative to the usual Royal Wulff.

Hook: Long-shank dry-fly hook, sizes 14 to 4.
Thread: Tan 3/0.
Tail: Amherst pheasant tippet.
Body: Hare's mask dubbing.
Wing: White calftail and pearl Krystal Flash.
Legs: Brown rubber legs.
Collar & head: Deer hair.

Power Ant

tied by Guy Turck
Jackson, Wyoming

Hook: Regular dry-fly hook, sizes 14 to 4.
Thread: Black 3/0.
Body: Black rabbit fur dubbing.
Wing: White calftail.
Legs: White rubber legs.
Hackle: Brown or furnace.
Head: Brown rabbit fur dubbing.

The Power Ant is sort of the little brother to Turck's Tarantula; the similarities are pretty obvious. Designed to imitate an ant, this fly catches trout when fished floating or even drawn under the water. It also works during a stonefly hatch or when grasshoppers fill the adjoining fields. It's a good light-line fly, and works very well with a 4- through 6-weight rod.

B.D.E. (Best Dry Ever) Green Drake

tied by Ben Furimsky
Crested Butte, Colorado

Hook: Regular dry-fly hook, sizes 10 and 8.
Thread: Rust 6/0.
Tail: Brown calftail.
Abdomen: Olive closed-cell foam.
Thorax: Peacock herl.
Hackle: Olive and dun.
Wing: Dun polypropylene yarn.

Ben tied this fly to match the western green drake. He begins by tying the tails and abdomen on a needle. He then slips the abdomen from the needle, ties it to the top of the hook shank, and completes the fly. This method creates a realistic, durable, high-floating dry fly.

Try this fly midday throughout June and July. It works best when fished with a dead-drift presentation.

Murray's Mr. Rapidan

tied by Harry Murray
Edinburg, Virginia

Hook: Regular dry-fly hook, sizes 20 to 12.
Thread: Tan 6/0.
Tail: Moose body hair.
Body: Quill Gordon Fly Rite dubbing.
Wing: Yellow calftail.
Hackle: Grizzly and brown.

Harry Murray is the fly-fishing sage of the Blue Ridge Mountains. He is vastly experienced in fishing for Virginia's native brook trout and smallmouth bass. Murray's Mr. Rapidan is an excellent general imitation of a quill Gordon, March brown, *Baetis*, or yellow stonefly. It's also an excellent searching pattern for those times when nothing is hatching.

Murray's Mr. Rapidan is included in Umpqua Feather Merchants's catalog of flies. Harry reports that it is a best-selling pattern on the East Coast.

If you can tie a Royal Wulff, you'll be able to dress the Mr. Rapidan.

Mr. Rapidan Parachute

tied by Harry Murray
Edinburg, Virginia

Hook: Dry-fly hook, sizes 20 to 12.
Thread: Tan 6/0.
Tail: Moose body hair.
Body: Quill Gordon Fly Rite dubbing.
Wing: Yellow calftail.
Hackle: Grizzly and brown.

This is the parachute version of Harry Murray's standard Mr. Rapidan. Parachute patterns are particularly effective near the beginning of a hatch. The insects' bodies hang down in the surface film, and the trout often key in on these emergers. The parachute pattern, with the hackle wrapped around the base of the wing, allows the body to nestle down in the surface film and mimic an emerging insect.

Harry uses this pattern in sizes 12 and 14 to match the March brown and quill Gordon hatches; he drops down to sizes 18 and 20 to match the blue-wing olive.

You can select a wide range of tackle to fish the standard and parachute Mr. Rapidan. These flies are delightful when fished with a short, 2-weight rod; the perfect outfit for native mountain brookies. If you fish larger rivers where you might encounter wind and bigger fish, step up to a 5- or 6-weight rod. Murray prefers using a 9-foot-long leader with a 4X to 7X tippet.

Hook: Alec Jackson Dee Low-Water Hook, size 9.
Thread: Hot orange Pearsall's Gossamer silk.
Egg sack: Black closed-cell foam.
Underbody: Rust closed-cell foam.
Body: Grizzly hair underfur dyed orange.
Overbody: Rust closed-cell foam.
Wing: Grizzly bear hair.
Legs: Small rubber legs.

Undertaker™

tied by Ken Burkholder
Boise, Idaho

"This fly is the finest salmon-fly pattern I have ever tied," says Ken Burkholder. "It utilizes grizzly bear hair for the wing. Grizzly bear has two qualities that deer, elk, moose, and squirrel utterly lack. The first is kinkiness. Bear hair traps air like no other material, creating flies with unparalleled floatation—perfect for the skittering presentation critical for pushing skeptical trout over the edge.

"Second, bear hair possesses a natural sheen that reflects light in a unique manner, imparting motion and 'winginess' that naturally mimics the fluttering of adult stoneflies. Sad, but true, I have caught gulls and robins on my bear-hair flies. They fool even birds."

Burkholder's Undertaker™, not to be confused with the hair-wing Atlantic salmon wet fly of the same name (which, curiously enough, is tied with black bear hair), is a great pattern to use during the hatches of the legendary salmon-fly stoneflies. This pattern, tied with closed-cell foam, is virtually unsinkable.

Red Bug

tied by Ken Burkholder
Boise, Idaho

Fish this big Royal Coachman variant during grasshopper season or when the big stoneflies are popping. Ken Burkholder recommends fishing this pattern and his Undertaker™ with a loop knot to increase their movement on the surface of the water.

"This fly was a new creation for 2002," says Burkholder. "It is similar to a Royal Coachman or a Red Ant. The difference is the moose-hair tail, the rubber legs, and the grizzly bear hair wing. Brown trout have a preference for this fly. I don't know how many three- to five-pound trout I've fooled with this pattern. Fish it during the salmonfly hatch and check it out."

Ken applies the Ice Dubbing in a dubbing loop, and coats the silk-thread abdomen with epoxy. Both of these practices make this pattern much more durable than a standard Royal Wulff.

Hook: Alec Jackson Dee River Low-Water Hook, size 9.
Thread: Scarlet Pearsall's Gossamer Silk.
Tail: Moose hair.
Butt: Peacock Ice Dubbing.
Abdomen: Tying thread.
Wing: Grizzly bear underfur.
Thorax: Peacock Ice Dubbing.
Hackle: Furnace.
Legs: Small rubber legs.

Hook: Tiemco TMC102y, sizes 15 and 13.
Thread: Olive Pearsall's Gossamer Silk.
Butt: Fine sulphur-orange dubbing.
Body: Fine pale-morning-dun dubbing.
Wing: Grizzly bear underfur.
Head: Fine olive dubbing.

Neapolitan PMD Bhaddis (Bear Hair Caddis)

tied by Ken Burkholder
Boise, Idaho

On his Undertaker™ and Red Bug, Ken Burkholder ties a fairly bushy wing; on this pattern, he scales back the use of bear hair for the wing. The Neapolitan PMD Bhaddis has been used to match hatches of yellow sallies and sulphur duns across the country. This pattern is simple to tie, and the kinky bear underfur keeps it afloat.

Ken has spent much of his life living and fishing in the Boise area. He grew up in Boise, and began fly fishing on Lime Creek, a tributary of the South Fork. He eventually shifted his focus to the bigger waters—the Middle Fork of the Boise, the South Fork of the Boise, the Big Wood River, Silver Creek, and ultimately the South Fork of the Snake River—where he has guided for over seventeen years.

Orange Sulphur Deer Hair Dun

tied by Ken Burkholder
Boise, Idaho

Like many guides, Ken Burkholder likes to fish tandem rigs (fish with two or more flies at the same time). A common arrangement is to tie a nymph or wet fly to a length of tippet, and attach the other end of the tippet to a floating fly. In addition to attracting its share of fish, the surface fly also acts as a strike indicator for the sub-surface pattern. Sometimes you can fish two floating flies at the same time. This is what Ken does with his Neapolitan PMD Bhaddis and Orange Sulphur Deer Hair Dun.

"The Neapolitan PMD Bhaddis fished in tandem with the Orange Sulphur Deer Hair Dun in riffle situations during 'prime time' on the South Fork affords the angler with opportunities for trout eating yellow sallies and emerging mayflies. If I had only two flies for the riffles during this time of the year, it would be these two."

Hook: Daiichi 1180, sizes 18 and 16.
Thread: Hot orange Pearsall's Gossamer Silk.
Tail: Gold Z-Lon.
Body: Tying thread.
Wing: Bleached deer hair.
Head: Fine sulphur-orange dubbing.

Hook: Orvis 122J, size 8.
Thread: Antique-gold Pearsall's Gossamer Silk.
Body: Bronze peacock herl.
Rib: Gold tying silk.
Hackle: Brown, honey dun, or furnace.
Wing: Grizzly bear underfur.
Over rib: Fine copper wire.

Peacock Bear Hair Golden Stone

tied by Ken Burkholder
Boise, Idaho

Ken Burkholder has developed several excellent patterns for matching the famed salmonfly hatch. His Peacock Bear Hair Golden Stone is another example. This pattern is smaller than his Undertaker™ and Red Bug, and is designed to match the male salmon fly and most golden stoneflies.

"This fly is unparalleled for imitating both the smaller male salmonfly, as well as the golden stonefly," says Burkholder. "Typically, the golden stonefly is slightly smaller than the salmonfly. This is why the patterns are generally smaller. But there is another good reason to fish a smaller pattern. Copulating stoneflies involve the 'salmon' fly, or the orange colored larger insect, but the smaller males are darker and often confused with golden stones. Not only will this pattern imitate the true golden stonefly (*Acroneuria californica*), but the male salmonfly (*Pteronarcys californica*)."

Ken Burkholder is a man of many talents. During the winter, he plays oboe in the Boise Philharmonic Orchestra. He received his degree in music from Northeastern University in 1984. Ken says that his ability to carve oboe reeds allows him to be very exacting when tying flies.

"For the last seventeen years, flies have taken a top priority in my guiding program. There are specific patterns I have developed that are simply more effective than standard shop flies. The flies I'm sharing with you afford the angler the best opportunity for dry-fly fishing during the last week of June through the first week of August. This is prime time—the finest fishing of the year. All fly fishermen should have these flies in their arsenals."

Kashner Rusty Spinner

tied by Chuck Kashner
Pawlet, Vermont

Hook: Mustad 94840, sizes 16 to 10.
Thread: Brown or olive 6/0.
Egg sac: Yellow dubbing.
Tails: Dark dun Microfibbetts.
Body: Rust dry-fly dubbing.
Rib: One strand of black sewing thread.
Wings: Mallard flank feathers.
Legs: Light dun dry-fly hackle.
Head: Rust dry-fly dubbing.

To create the wings, Chuck Kashner ties on the mallard flank feathers, and uses a series of figure-eight wraps to splay them into the spent position. He then ties on the hackle, and adds a pinch of dubbing to the thread. Next, he makes a couple of figure-eight wraps of dubbing around the wing tie-in point; this creates a thin thorax. To complete the fly, he wraps the hackle on the dubbed thorax, and makes a small dubbed head.

"I normally use this fly in the evening in May, June, and September," says Kashner. "Generally, when the fish are rising in an unhurried but rhythmic manner, they are taking the spent spinners. This is one of my favorite spinners for calm pools right after dark."

Ausable Wulff

tied by Fran Betters
Wilmington, New York

Hook: Regular dry-fly hook, sizes 18 to 8.
Thread: Red 8/0.
Tail: Woodchuck hair.
Body: Rusty-orange Australian opossum dubbing.
Wing: White calftail.
Hackle: Brown and grizzly.

Fran Betters is a legend of the Adirondack Mountains and the Ausable River. I met him at his shop, the Adirondack Sports Shop, which has been in business since 1964. It just so happened that I stopped by the shop the evening he was having one of his regular barbecues for his friends and customers. It was a wonderful time and a great chance to meet some of the local anglers.

One of the nice things about fishing the Ausable is that there is very little development along the river, and there is ample access to very long stretches of water. It's fairly easy to find a place to fish where you'll rarely see another angler.

Fran recommends his Ausable Wulff for fishing throughout the season, and at any time of the day. It is an excellent attractor pattern, but also works to imitate a wide variety of hatching mayflies. This bushy pattern stays afloat on the turbulent sections of the Ausable—and there are a lot turbulent areas.

Fran still ties all of the Ausable Wulffs sold at his store—over 5,000 a year!

Hook: Regular dry-fly hook, sizes 16 to 10.
Thread: Red 8/0.
Tail: Natural deer-hair tips.
Body: Brown dry-fly dubbing.
Wing: Natural deer-hair tips.

Haystack

tied by Fran Betters
Wilmington, New York

The Haystack features an economy of materials, and is another demonstration that sometimes the simplest patterns work the best. Fran Betters designed the Haystack to imitate an emerging caddisfly.

Note that the deer-hair wing is tied splayed. This method allows the deer-hair tips to act like hackle and hold the fly on the surface of the water. Fran developed his Haystack series of flies in the 1940s, and these became the basis for the popular patterns known as Comparaduns.

The Usual

tied by Fran Betters
Wilmington, New York

This is another of Fran Better's famous flies. Again, it is very basic and requires only a couple of materials. Fran's patterns prove the adage that sometimes (maybe most of the time) simple really is better. Bill Phillips, a close friend of Fran's, was the first to test the fly that would eventually become known as the Usual. Bill had such great success with the fly that he was soon using it almost exclusively. Whenever another angler would ask him what fly he was using, he would respond, "the usual." The name stuck.

Fran Better's Adirondack Sports Shop has a long, illustrious history in modern Ausable River fly-fishing history. Fran began operating his shop in 1964, and it quickly became a Mecca for anglers fishing the river. Other shops have opened, but the parking lot at Fran's always seems to be a bit fuller with cars. In addition to carrying Fran's flies, the shop also offers a complete line of custom-made rods.

Hook: Regular dry-fly hook, sizes 18 to 12.
Thread: Pink 8/0.
Tail: The fur from the bottom of a snow-shoe hare's foot.
Body: Tan fine dubbing.
Wing: The fur from the bottom of a snow-shoe hare's foot.

Hook: Regular dry-fly hook, sizes 18 to 10.
Thread: Tan 6/0.
Tail: Brown hackle fibers.
Body: Natural hare's mask dubbing.
Wing post: White calftail.
Hackle: Brown and grizzly.

Parachute Hare's Ear

tied by Jay Buchner
Jackson, Wyoming

What can I say about Jay Buchner? He contributed an article to the first issue of *Fly Tyer* magazine over twenty-five years ago, and continues to be a regular contributor to that magazine. He is a regular guide in the Jackson Hole One Fly Tournament, and he is member of the team representing the United States to the annual International Fly Fishing Championships. That's a pretty full resume.

Jay uses the Parachute Hare's Ear from July through October. For tying the fly, he recommends placing the wing post near the middle of the hook shank for better balance and floatation. He also wraps the hackle around the wing post in a counterclockwise direction. This is key because the feather and the thread will be going in the same direction when you tie off the hackle.

Jay's Stonefly

tied by Jay Buchner
Jackson, Wyoming

There's nothing like when the big stoneflies hatch on Jay Buchner's home Western rivers. The fishing is fast and exciting, and you'll need large dry flies that remain afloat. Jay fishes this pattern with a 6- or 7-weight rod, and intersperses a dead-drift presentation with slight twitches to simulate a struggling adult stonefly.

Jay ties the first half of the fly using size 3/0 thread, but switches to size A for spinning the deer hair head. He spins two clumps of deer hair to create the full, high-floating collar and head. He also clips the bottom of the head flat to maintain the wide hook gap.

Hook: Atlantic salmon dry-fly salmon hook, sizes 10 to 4.
Thread: Pale yellow 3/0.
Tail: Elk mane.
Body: Pale yellow or orange polypropylene yarn.
Rib: Badger or brown saddle hackle, spiral-wrapped over the body.
Wing: Elk mane.
Collar & head: Deer hair, spun and clipped to shape.

Gray Trude

tied by Jay Buchner
Jackson, Wyoming

Hook: Regular dry-fly hook, sizes 18 to 8.
Thread: Gray 6/0 or 3/0.
Tail: Grizzly hackle fibers.
Body: Medium gray dubbing.
Wing: White calftail.
Hackle: Grizzly.

The Trude series of flies are excellent attractor patterns. They can be used anytime of the year when the trout are striking dry flies. The gray Trude is a long-time favorite that can be used to search the water, and will even work to match many species of mayflies.

Jay Buchner fishes the Gray Trude dead-drift, and will sometimes twitch it across the surface. He also uses it as the floating anchor fly in a tandem-fly rig.

Gray Paradrake

tied by Jay Buchner
Jackson, Wyoming

Hook: Regular dry-fly hook, size 12.
Thread: Gray 3/0.
Tails: Six moose hairs.
Wing post: Dark deer hair.
Body: Elk hair dyed gray, and .015-inch-diameter monofilament for the underbody.
Hackle: Grizzly saddle hackle.

Here's what Jay Buchner has to say about tying his Gray Paradrake:

"Tie the elk hair in reverse in front of the wing and pull it back around the wing. Spiral-wrap the tying thread back around the elk hair down the hook shank and out onto the monofilament underbody to make the extended body. The body should extend about a shank length past the end of the hook. Secure the end of the extended body with a couple of wraps, and then spiral-wrap the thread forward. Tie on the hackle and wrap counterclockwise. To finish the fly, clip the monofilament and the excess elk hairs. Leave three moose hairs for the tails."

Jay fishes the Gray Paradrake from June through August, and it is a particularly good imitation of the gray drake.

Pheasant-Tail Variant

tied by Gloria Jordan
Manchester Center, Vermont

It's a great pleasure to include Gloria Jordan's flies in this book. Mrs. Jordan is the wife of the late Wes Jordan, the head rodmaker for the Orvis Company. Wes created unique methods for producing large numbers of really high quality bamboo rods, and also developed a patented impregnation process. Today, Orvis rods made during the Jordan years are very collectible, and rods baring Wes's signature are particularly desirable.

Gloria has operated a fly shop on the outskirts of Manchester, Vermont, the home of Orvis, for many years.

Hook: Mustad 94840, sizes 18 to 12.
Thread: Black 6/0.
Tail: Brown Microfibbetts.
Body: Pheasant tail fibers.
Rib: Fine gold wire.
Hackle: Furnace.

Rob's 100-Pound Coffin Fly

tied by Robert Lewis
Pound Ridge, New York

Hook: Curved-shank scud hook, size 12.
Thread: Black 6/0.
Tail: Three white Microfibbetts.
Abdomen: 100-pound-test monofilament coated with Softex and covered with Antron.
Thorax: Black tying thread.
Wing post: White Antron.

Rob Lewis designed the prototype of this fly in a campground in Roscoe, New York. He had been fishing the local coffin-fly hatch, and wanted a better imitation of this important insect. The Antron he used for the wing was a piece of stuffing from the seat of his Honda automobile.

The Super Sally

tied by Justin Moeykens
New Boston, New Hampshire

Hook: Tiemco TMC2312, sizes 16 to 10.
Thread: Chartreuse 6/0.
Body: Bright green dubbing.
Hackle: Cream.
Wing: Bleached coastal deer hair.

This trout pattern is an excellent imitation of the yellow Sally stonefly, a commonly available summer insect that hatches during early summer. Note that Justin Moeykens dubs the body very thin, and wraps the hackle thick and bushy. He also says that the fly's light color "makes it a perfect last fly of the day when seeing your fly on the water is most difficult."

Fish the Super Sally upstream with a dead-drift presentation. If that doesn't work, try skating the fly across the surface. The pattern's heavy hackle keeps the fly afloat and attracts the fish that are feeding on the real stoneflies that are flitting on the surface.

Trico Spinner

tied by Rick Murphy
Colorado Springs, Colorado

"I use this fly from July through September during the Trico hatch. I use a smaller fly as the season progresses. Also, use it during the later stages of the hatch with a little weight and fish it as a drowned spinner. You can fish this pattern either dry or sunken."

Hook: Tiemco TMC100, sizes 24 to 20.
Thread: Black 8/0.
Tails: Light dun or white Microfibbetts.
Abdomen: Black tying thread.
Wings: White Antron.
Thorax: Black Superfine dubbing or peacock herl.

Hook: Tiemco TMC100, sizes 26 to 18.
Thread: Black 8/0.
Tail: Brown and grizzly hackle fibers.
Body: Adams gray Superfine Dubbing.
Wing post: White calftail or Superfine dubbing.
Hackle: Grizzly and brown.

Parachute Adams

tied by Rick Murphy
Colorado Springs, Colorado

"We use this pattern from February through November to match the blue-winged olives and midges. I fish it dry, and sometimes tail it behind a floating fly as an emerger. Also, trim one side of the parachute and fish it as a cripple."

Mac's Cicada

tied by Mac McGee
Chattanooga, Tennessee

Hook: Dry-fly hook, sizes 8 and 6.
Thread: Black 6/0.
Tail: Wood duck flank fibers.
Body: Peacock colored dubbing.
Wing: White bucktail with strands of pearl Flashabou.
Legs: Olive/black Sili Legs with flakes.
Head: Deer body hair dyed olive.

Mac's Cicada is a variation of Turk's Tarantula, a pattern that is a favorite in the annual Jackson Hole One Fly competition. The Tarantula, and the Cicada, are great attractor dry flies, and are especially good selections to fish during grasshopper season. Mac had very good luck using his Cicada on New Zealand's South Island.

CDC Caddis

tied by Tim Savard
Pittsburgh, New Hampshire

Hook: Regular dry-fly hook, sizes 20 to 14.
Thread: Gray, olive or rust brown 8/0.
Body: Gray, olive, or rust brown Superfine dubbing.
Wing: Cul de canard.

According to Tim Savard, tier Dan Fitzgerald developed the CDC Caddis for fishing on the Kennebago River. It's a simple pattern designed for catching trout and landlocked salmon. It's also a very dainty fly, and can be cast with the lightest tackle.

After making the body, Tim ties on three CDC feathers. He then clips the feathers to length—"about one-third again longer than the body."

A word about Lopstick Lodge. Tim and Lisa run a great operation. The cabins are clean and comfortable, and the fishing in northern New Hampshire is outstanding. The headwaters of the Connecticut River run between a series of lakes, and offer trout and landlocked salmon. The area is accessible but remote; there is little development, and the scenery is wonderful. I always enjoy fishing the upper Connecticut River, and am looking forward to my next trip. I am very happy to recommend Lopstick Lodge.

Hook: Regular dry-fly hook, sizes 20 and 18.
Thread: Light tan 8/0.
Body: Fluorescent chartreuse Superfine dubbing.
Wing: Light tan cul de canard feathers.

CDC Sally

tied by Tim Savard
Pittsburgh, New Hampshire

The CDC Sally is a variation of the CDC Caddis. This pattern is designed to match the yellow Sally stonefly hatch. This is an important hatch throughout the North Woods, and the CDC Sally is a good imitation. The fly is lightweight, and the CDC feathers keep the fly afloat. Tim and Lisa Savard fish this pattern with dead-drift presentations and 3- to 5-weight rods.

Old Blind Man Beetle

tied by Barry Staats
Media, Pennsylvania

Barry is a longtime friend. He owns a great shop in Media, a town right next to Philadelphia. I've always liked the name of his establishment: The Sporting Gentleman. Back in the days when I made and sold split-bamboo fly rods, Barry was one of the first fly shops to carry my rods. I've always appreciated his interest in my work.

Barry is a well-respected fly fisherman in eastern Pennsylvania. In the year 2000, the National Republican Party held its presidential convention in Philadelphia. As part of the entertainment, a fly-fishing trip to Valley Forge was offered to the conventioneers. A group of delegates jumped at the chance, including Speaker of the House of Representatives, Dennis Hastart. Barry Staats played a key role in planning the trip.

Barry says he developed the Old Blind Man "about ten years ago when my eyes started to fail me and I was having trouble seeing dark flies on the water and I was missing strikes. This problem prompted me to consider ways to make hard-to-see flies more visible. The first Old Blind Man I developed was a foam beetle. I tied this fly with chartreuse Fly Foam and used a black permanent marker to paint the underside of the body. The Old Blind Man concept has now expanded to include a whole series of flies."

The Old Blind Man Beetle is a good terrestrial pattern. He recommends using a rod matched with a 3- to 5-weight line, and a 9-foot, 4X to 6X leader. This fly catches trout throughout the year, from spring to first frost. Barry casts the Old Blind Man Beetle under trees and against the bank, and fishes it with a dead-drift.

Hook: Regular dry-fly hook, sizes 18 to 12.
Thread: Black 6/0.
Body: Chartreuse Fly Foam.
Legs: Stiff terrestrial leg material.

Mr. Rapidan Ant

tied by Harry Murray
Edinburg, Virginia

Hook: Regular dry-fly hook, sizes 22 to 12.
Thread: Black 6/0.
Wing: Yellow calftail.
Body: Fine black dubbing.
Hackle: Grizzly.

"When fishing for trout on flat water, this pattern is tough to beat," says Harry Murray. This fly is especially good during midsummer when ants become an important terrestrial source of food for the fish. The bright yellow wing makes it especially easy to see on the water.

Harry Murray is a noted fly-fishing authority. He is the author of a half-dozen books, and is a member of the Outdoor Writers Association of America and the Virginia Outdoor Writers Association. Harry has appeared in instructional videos, and has taught fly tying and fishing across the country.

Murray's Flying Beetle

tied by Harry Murray
Edinburg, Virginia

Hook: Regular dry-fly hook, sizes 20 to 14.
Thread: Black 6/0.
Body: Peacock herl.
Wing: Light elk hair.
Legs: Black deer hair.

This is another of Harry Murray's great terrestrial patterns. Use it during the summer wherever terrestrials are important to the fish—and the fishermen.

"This is my most successful fly on spring creeks and mountain streams from June through November when there are no hatches," says Murray.

Fishing Murray's Flying Beetle is an especially fun fly for light-tackle enthusiasts. Fish this fly using a long, lightweight leader, and take care to use a drag-free presentation. Also try fishing the Flying Beetle with slight twitches to imitate a struggling beetle. This pattern works on Pennsylvania's limestone streams, Montana's spring creeks, and dozens of streams in between.

MiscreAnt

tied by Dusty Wissmath
Raven Rocks, Virginia

Guide Dusty Wissmath designed this pattern to imitate a carpenter ant, an important midsummer terrestrial source of food for eastern trout. He fishes this pattern in the heat of the summer from midmorning throughout the afternoon when the real ants are most active and likely to fall onto the water.

Wissmath begins the fly by tying in a small bunch of black deer hair on top of the hook (tie the tips of the hairs to the hook). Next, wrap Flashabou over the bound-down deer-hair tips and halfway up the hook shank. Pull the deer hair over the top of the fly and tie down. Wrap the front half of the shank with thread. Pull the deer hair forward and tie off to form the front half of the body; pull a few hairs out to the sides of the fly to create the legs. Clip the deer hair head and legs to length.

Dusty Wissmath has been fly fishing for close to forty years, and is a member of the Scott Fly Rod, Ross Reels, and Hyde Drift Boat pro staffs. He attended the University of Wyoming, and after graduate school began guiding on the Snake, Firehole, Madison and Yellowstone Rivers. Dusty moved to Virginia about twelve years ago.

Hook: Regular dry-fly hook, sizes 14 to 8.
Thread: Black 3/0.
Body: Pearl Flashabou.
Back & legs: Black deer hair.

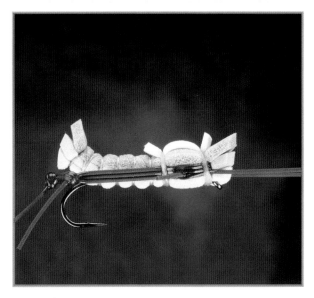

Club Sandwich®

tied by Ken Burkholder
Boise, Idaho

Hook: 4X-long light-wire hook, sizes 8 and 6.
Thread: Primrose yellow Pearsall's Gossamer Thread.
Body: A combination of light Cahill, flesh, gray or tan closed-cell foam.
Legs: Brown rubber legs.
Strike indicator: White closed-cell foam.

Every Western trout angler needs a selection of grasshopper patterns. The Club Sandwich® is Ken Burkholder's entry into this fun category of flies. And yes, the name of this pattern really is registered.

"This is my best known fly," Burkholder commented. "In 1999, Carter Andrews fished this fly in the Jackson Hole One Fly. It enabled him to wrap up the professional division for the contest. It is registered with the United States Patent and Trademark Office with registration number 2,536,398. This fly became extremely popular and was knocked off by many fly manufacturers under different names, or buy them through Umpqua Feather Merchants, the exclusive licensed tier for this pattern."

I.C.S.I. (I Can See It) Ant

tied by Thomas Baltz
Mt. Holly Springs, Pennsylvania

Hook: Daiichi 1180 or 1100, sizes 16 and 14.
Thread: Black 6/0.
Body: Black dubbing.
Wing post: Hot orange calftail.
Hackle: Grizzly.

This fly is my version of a design shown to me by the late Dr. Jack Beck, of Carlisle, Pennsylvania. I consider the bright calftail wing and grizzly hackle to be the most important features and not just variations. I prefer the calftail to synthetic materials because the hair is stiffer, making it easier to wind the parachute hackle.

"The hackle is particularly important. Most parachute ant patterns seem to use black or brown hackle, both of which obscure the silhouette of the body. The grizzly hackle allows the body shape to show through.

"Placing the post between the humps is also important. It makes a more balanced fly, allowing it to float better than ants with the post and hackle emanating from the front hump."

Slickwater Damsel Nymph

tied by Rob McLean
Rawlins, Wyoming

Hook: Long-shank nymph hook, sizes 12 to 8.
Thread: Olive or tan, 6/0 or 8/0.
Tail: Marabou.
Abdomen: Stripped quill, wrapped on the hook and coated with head cement.
Thorax: Dubbing.
Wing case: Tyvek clipped to shape and colored with a waterproof marker.
Eyes: Melted monofilament.
Legs: Mallard flank.

Here's another fly that can be used in most regions of country. All ponds, lakes, and slow-moving streams with silted bottoms have damselflies; if these are the kinds of waters you fish, you'll want to carry the Slickwater Damsel Nymph. Select materials in colors to match real damselfly larvae. The Slickwater Damsel Nymph is lightweight and works well with a 4- or 5-weight outfit, making it a real pleasure to cast.

Iowa Mystery Nymph

tied by Scott Sickau
Boone, Iowa

Hook: Daiichi 1710, sizes 16 to 12.
Thread: Black 8/0.
Tail: Mallard flank dyed yellow.
Abdomen: Tan or light cream fur dubbing.
Rib: Fine copper wire or one strand of pearl Krystal Flash.
Thorax: Tan or light cream dubbing.

The Iowa Mystery Nymph is used to catch warmwater species, and will also do a number on trout. Scott Sickau says this pattern is a good imitation of Iowa's March brown mayflies—which it is—but it will match a number of mayfly nymphs.

Joe's Black Caddis

tied by Scott Sickau
Boone, Iowa

Hook: Daiichi 1150, sizes 18 to 12.
Thread: Black 14/0.
Head: Black tungsten bead, sized to match the hook.
Tail: A small tuft of black marabou.
Body: Black dubbing.
Rib: Narrow copper wire.
Wings: Two natural mallard flank biots.

Scott Sickau says that this Colorado trout pattern is a good imitation of a little black sedge. He uses this pattern throughout the summer, and it works any time of the day. He fishes it with a fine, 6X tippet.

Yellow Stonefly

tied by Scott Sickau
Boone, Iowa

Hook: Daiichi 1270, sizes 20 to 4.
Thread: Black 8/0.
Tail & antennae: Black goose biots.
Body: Yellow craft foam.
Legs: Natural grizzly hackle stems.

Many rivers have populations of yellow stonefly nymphs. They come in a wide range of sizes, and Sickau's Yellow Stonefly can be tied in sizes that match them all.

After tying on the foam body, use a brown permanent marker to give the fly realistic stripes and bars.

Mr. Rapidan Bead-head Nymph

tied by Harry Murray
Edinburg, Virginia

Harry Murray owns a fly shop in Edinburg, Virginia. His establishment is called, appropriately enough, Murray's Fly Shop. In addition to a complete line of fishing tackle and tying materials and tools, Murray's Fly Shop offers a full schedule of classes. Murray's Fly Shop is a central gathering place for anglers who fish the Blue Ridge and surrounding area.

The Mr. Rapidan Bead-head Nymph is a good general pattern for imitating a wide variety of mayfly nymphs. Follow basic nymph-tying techniques, but use Murray's list of materials to create this fly.

Hook: Regular nymph hook, sizes 18 to 10.
Head: Small brass bead.
Thread: Tan 6/0.
Tail: Ring-necked pheasant tail fibers.
Body: Hare's ear dubbing.
Rib: Fine copper wire.
Wing: Mallard breast feather.
Legs: Tan hen hackle.

Hook: 4X-long nymph hook, sizes 14 to 6, straight or bent to shape.
Thread: Tan 6/0 or 8/0.
Tail: Tan goose biots.
Abdomen: A blend of dubbing: buff fox, brown rabbit, and tan Antron.
Rib: Narrow brown Vinyl Rib followed by narrow gold tinsel.
Thorax: Same dubbing as the abdomen.
Legs: Brown or dark ginger hen hackle.
Wing case: Oak turkey.

Tan Stonefly Nymph

tied by Tony Mastaler
Springfield, Vermont

Tony Mastaler is guiding in middle Vermont, specializing in the Williams, Black, White, and upper Connecticut Rivers. All of this offers excellent fly fishing. He uses his Tan Stonefly Nymph throughout much of the day from spring through early July. He uses the typical upstream, dead-drift approach, and tries to keep the fly near the bottom.

Yellow Stonefly Nymph

tied by Tony Mastaler
Springfield, Vermont

Mastaler's Yellow Stonefly Nymph is a good choice to match the common yellow and lime Sally nymphs. It would also work during a hatch of sulphur mayflies. This fly is expertly tied, and a good example for all novices interested in dressing small nymphs.

Tony Mastaler guides out of Springfield, Vermont. In addition to the fine local fishing, Springfield is also the home of the Springfield Telescope Makers. The Springfield Telescope Makers owns a large piece of property that is the home of their permanent observatory. Every summer, the club holds an event called Stellafane, which is the world's largest gathering of amateur telescope makers. I've attended several Stellafanes, and they are always great events. There are programs that appeal to star-gazing fans of all levels of expertise, as well as plenty of activities to keep the kids busy. I can't recommend Stellafane highly enough.

Hook: 4X-long nymph hook, sizes 16 to 10, straight or bent to shape.
Thread: Yellow 6/0 or 8/0.
Tail: Yellow goose biots.
Abdomen: A blend of dubbing: cream fox, light yellow rabbit, and yellow Antron.
Rib: Narrow yellow Vinyl Rib followed by gold wire.
Thorax: Same dubbing as the abdomen.
Legs: Light ginger hen hackle.
Wing case: Oak turkey.

Hook: Mustad 9671, sizes 12 and 10.
Thread: Claret 6/0.
Tail: Peacock sword fibers.
Body: Peacock herl with one strand of cream sewing thread down the back.
Rib: Copper wire.
Wing case: Wild turkey back feather.
Hackle: Brown hen hackle.

Kashner Iso-Nymph

tied by Chuck Kashner
Pawlet, Vermont

This is one of Chuck Kashner's favorite flies for fishing faster water where you'll find real *Isonychia* mayfly nymphs.

"I generally fish this pattern down and across in fast or even white water. It is very important to let this fly swing into the bank. *Isonychia* nymphs crawl out of the water onto the rocks to hatch, so if they are present you will see their cases on the rocks along the shore. This fly can produce big fish, and the hits to it are always hard."

Kashner prefers fishing this pattern in the fall—from late August through October—and from late morning until dark.

Chuck Kashner is an Orvis endorsed guide in southern Vermont. He takes his client's to rivers, streams, lakes, and ponds to fish for trout, landlocked salmon, lake trout, bass, and pike.

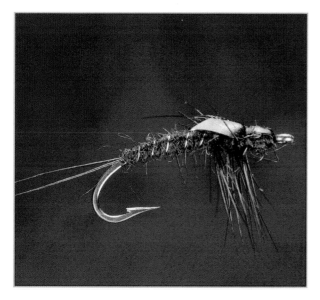

Black Stonefly Nymph

tied by Ron Kozlowski
Nicholson, Pennsylvania

Hook: Bent-shank nymph hook, sizes 16 to 112.
Thread: Black 14/0.
Tail: Moose body hair.
Abdomen: Black dubbing.
Rib: Copper wire.
Thorax: Black dubbing.
Wing pad & head: Black Thin Skin.

Ron Kozlowski has been guiding for over twenty-five years. He takes clients to Pennsylvania's South Branch of the Tunkannock, Lackawanna, and Delaware Rivers, where you can find "great stonefly hatches starting in March."

Pheasant-Tail Nymph

tied by Thomas Baltz
Mt. Holly Springs, Pennsylvania

Hook: Daiichi 1560, sizes 20 to 14.
Thread: Fine copper wire, coated red.
Tail, body, & wing case: Ringed-neck-pheasant tail fibers.

Tom Baltz says "this nymph, designed by the late Frank Sawyer, is the premier 'sight fishing' nymph, and was developed by Mr. Sawyer to fish the River Avon in southern England, where he was the river-keeper for many years. I have found it an extremely effective fly anywhere I have used it. If you can see the trout, you'll usually get a reaction if you cast the fly ahead of the fish and watch to see when the trout takes the fly. I adjust my tippet and the size of the fly based on the current speed and water depth to obtain the proper sink rate. Matching the size of the natural nymphs is sometimes a consideration, but the sink rate is my primary concern."

There are a lot of more realistic nymphs, but the Pheasant-Tail Nymph remains a standard. This pattern and the standard Hare's Ear Nymph probably account for more nymph-caught trout than all of the other patterns combined.

Hook: Daiichi 1180 or 1100, sizes 24 to 8.
Thread: Olive 6/0.
Tail: Olive brown Z-Lon.
Body: Hare's mask dubbing.
Wing post: Yellow or orange calftail.
Hackle: Grizzly.

ParaNymph

tied by Thomas Baltz
Mt. Holly Springs, Pennsylvania

The ParaNymph is a good candidate to try when the trout are feeding on emerging nymphs in the surface film. Tie this pattern in a variety of sizes and colors to match your local mayflies.

Tom shares his wisdom about tying and fishing:

"For many years I didn't use parachute style dry flies. They were not dry enough and did not seem to be good imitations of newly hatched duns. I still feel that way, but then I came up with the idea to use the parachute design to create an emerger. This pattern is intended to be a generic pattern to suggest a nymph or pupa drifting at the surface. This has become my most successful surface fly. It has been fished all over the world—but unfortunately not by me!

"I have had success with it as a searching fly, and also fished it during numerous hatches such as blue quills, Hendricksons, *Callibaetis*, sulphurs, pale morning duns, and blue-wing olives.

"I feel that size and shape are the two most important considerations when choosing a surface fly, with color a distant third. I wouldn't want to be caught on any stream in the world without a selection of these flies. I know there are some similar flies out there, but I did come up with this one on my own."

Isonychia Nymph

tied by Robert Lewis
Pound Ridge, New York

Isonychia mayflies are widespread across North America. The nymphs are excellent swimmers, and dart around the streambed. When they emerge, the nymphs swim quickly to the surface. Fish *Isonychia* nymph imitations down-and-across stream with short strips.

Robert Lewis uses his Isonychia Nymph on the Beaverkill, which has both the *Salederi* and Bi-color varieties of this mayfly.

Hook: 2X-long nymph hook, size 14.
Thread: Olive 6/0.
Tail: Three peacock sword fibers.
Abdomen: Three gray ostrich herls, tied to the hook, twisted together, and wrapped up the shank. Color the top of the fly with a black permanent marker.
Rib: Monofilament.
Thorax: Ostrich herl dyed olive.
Wing case: Pintail flank covered with Softex. The stripe on the wing case is made with a stripped hackle stem.
Legs: Hungarian partridge.

March Brown Nymph

tied by Robert Lewis
Pound Ridge, New York

Hook: Regular nymph or wet-fly hook, size 12.
Thread: Dark brown 6/0.
Tail: Three peccary fibers.
Underbody: Brown dubbing.
Side body: Yellow Ultra Chenille.
Rib: Brown tying thread.
Thorax: Gold hare's ear dubbing.
Wing case: Lemon wood duck stiffened with Softex.
Legs: Hungarian partridge fibers.

The March brown mayfly is widespread across North America, and Rob Lewis's March Brown Nymph is a good pattern to match the larva. Secure the yellow Ultra Chenille, which imitates the gills of the nymph, to the sides of the body with a rib of brown tying thread.

Black Stonefly Nymph

tied by Robert Lewis
Pound Ridge, New York

Hook: Mustad 9672, sizes 8 to 4.
Thread: Black 8/0.
Tails: Turkey biots dyed black.
Abdomen: Foam stretched and flattened, and colored with permanent markers to match the natural.
Legs: Turkey biots dyed black and knotted to form the leg joints.
Thorax: Black dubbing.
Wing case: Foam: stretched, flattened, and clipped to shape. Color the wing case with a black permanent marker.
Eyes: Melted monofilament.
Antennae: Stripped hackle quills dyed black.

Guide Robert Lewis ties an entire series of realistic stonefly nymphs. The legs on this imitation are particularly interesting. Creating the legs on realistic nymphs is always a challenge, and Robert has come up with a good solution. Tying a knot in the turkey biots creates passable leg joints. He then ties the knotted biots to the sides of the fly.

Drifting Golden Stonefly Nymph

tied by Robert Lewis
Pound Ridge, New York

Most stonefly nymph imitations are tied on straight-shank hooks, or hooks with slightly bent shanks. When a stonefly nymph is dislodged from the streambed and drifts in the current, it generally curls up very similar to Rob Lewis's Drifting Golden Stonefly Nymph. Check this out for yourself. The next time you go fishing, overturn some rocks and collect a few real golden stonefly nymphs. Release them in the current and watch how they drift. Most of the nymphs will quickly curl up and begin drifting, waiting to land on the bottom or bump into a log, rock, or other obstruction.

Robert uses an interesting method for creating the legs on this fly. Stonefly nymphs have fine filaments on their legs, and it's pretty tough to capture this feature on an imitation. Rob selects six partridge feathers for the legs. He then clips the fibers from each feather. Next, he heats a bodkin, and touches the middle of each feather quill with the bodkin. The stem will bend around the bodkin and form a jointed leg. Don't overheat the bodkin or it will burn through the quill. Work slowly and you'll get the hang of this technique. Yes, this is a time-consuming way to tie flies; spend an evening just making legs, and complete the flies the next day. I tie stonefly nymphs with these types of legs, and I use them to catch fish when no other fly works.

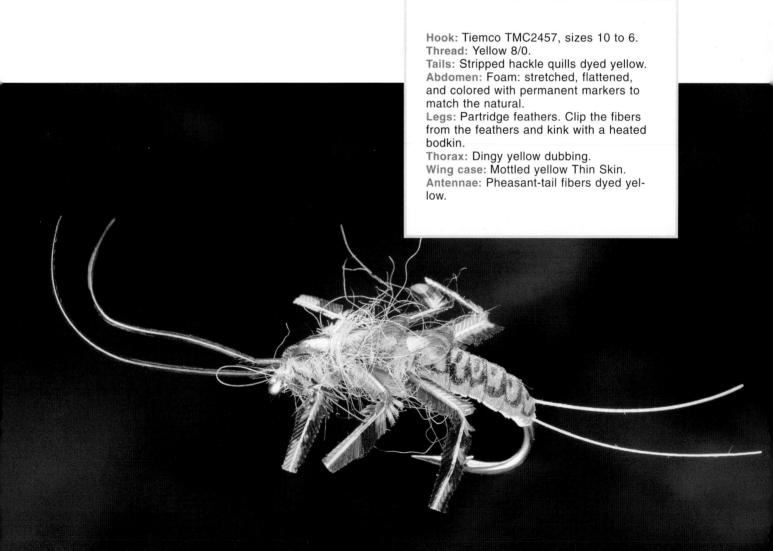

Hook: Tiemco TMC2457, sizes 10 to 6.
Thread: Yellow 8/0.
Tails: Stripped hackle quills dyed yellow.
Abdomen: Foam: stretched, flattened, and colored with permanent markers to match the natural.
Legs: Partridge feathers. Clip the fibers from the feathers and kink with a heated bodkin.
Thorax: Dingy yellow dubbing.
Wing case: Mottled yellow Thin Skin.
Antennae: Pheasant-tail fibers dyed yellow.

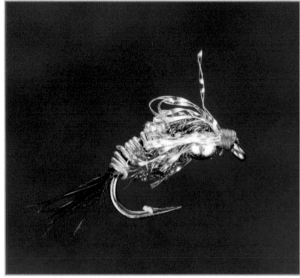

D.Y. Scud

tied by Justin Moeykens
New Boston, New Hampshire

Hook: Tiemco TMC2488, sizes 18 to 12.
Thread: Orange 6/0.
Tail: Orange Flouro Fiber.
Body: Ginger SLF dubbing.
Shellback: Ginger Thin Skin.
Rib: Orange ultraviolet Krystal Flash.
Antennae: Orange Flouro Fiber.

Scuds are common crustaceans in many tailwaters
and spring creeks—any stream rich in aquatic plant
life. If you walk the streambank slowly and quietly,
you might spot a trout digging in the plants and feeding on scuds. In many of these rivers, the fish grow
very large because of the steady food supply.

Fish the D.Y. Scud throughout the season with a
dead-drift presentation. If the water is deep, add a
couple of pieces of split shot to the leader; you'll want
to fish the D.Y. Scud near the bottom where the trout
are foraging for real scuds.

Bead-head Bubble-back Copper

tied by Rick Murphy
Colorado Springs, Colorado

Hook: Tiemco TMC2457, sizes 18 to 14.
Thread: Black 8/0 for tying the body, and rusty
brown 8/0 for tying the head.
Bead: Small silver or copper bead.
Tail: Rusty brown pheasant fibers.
Abdomen: Chartreuse wire (black or red wire will
also work).
Back & legs: Pearl Krystal Flash.
Thorax: Peacock herl or dubbing.
Wing case: Rusty brown pheasant-tail fibers.

Tie in all of the materials, and leave about an eighth
of an inch at the head to whip-finish the thread," says
Rick Murphy. "Tie on the rust thread and pull the
wing case over the top, and then pull over the Krystal
Flash for the bubble. Pull the legs down the sides and
finish the fly. Pull the Krystal Flash up a bit with the
tip of bodkin to get a slight bubble effect."

Use this fly to match midges as well as small mayflies
and caddisflies.

Micro Mayfly

tied by Rick Murphy
Colorado Springs, Colorado

This pattern, developed by Californian Mike Mercer, has become popular in Colorado for matching small mayfly nymphs. "We use this fly from March through October for matching blue-winged olives and pale morning duns," says Rick Murphy. "Dead-drift it along the bottom behind another fly as a midge or small emerger."

Hook: Tiemco TMC2487, sizes 20 to 16.
Thread: Olive or dun, size 8/0.
Head: Small silver bead.
Tail: Mallard fibers dyed rust.
Abdomen: Stripped peacock herl.
Rib: Extra-fine copper or silver wire.
Thorax: Gray or cream Superfine dubbing.
Wing case: Pearl Flashabou.
Legs: Partridge fibers.

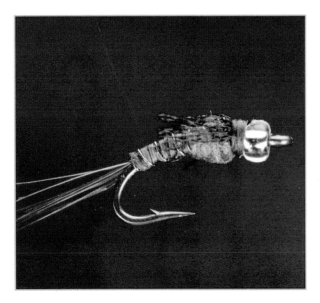

Bead-head Baetis

tied by Rick Murphy
Colorado Springs, Colorado

Hook: Tiemco TMC100, sizes 22 to 18.
Thread: Dun 8/0.
Head: Extra-small silver glass bead.
Tail: Olive brown hackle fibers.
Abdomen: Olive brown Superfine dubbing.
Rib: Extra-fine silver or copper wire.
Thorax: Olive brown Superfine dubbing.
Wing case & legs: Black Organza folded over the top to form the wing case, and pulled down the sides of the fly to make the legs.

Baetis mayflies are widespread, and must be matched using very small flies and "technical" fishing methods. Guide Rick Murphy says he uses his Bead-head Baetis from March through October to match blue-winged olive nymphs. He dead-drifts the fly below an emerger pattern, and picks up the trout that are keying in on the nymphs. This tiny pattern demands a fine leader, and Murphy relies on 6X fluorocarbon.

Flashback Peasant-Tail Nymph

tied by Rick Murphy
Colorado Springs, Colorado

Hook: Tiemco TMC100, sizes 22 to 18.
Thread: Brown 8/0.
Tail: Pheasant tail fibers.
Abdomen: Pheasant tail fibers wrapped up the hook.
Rib: Copper or red wire.
Thorax: Peacock herl.
Legs: Pheasant tail fibers.
Wing case: Pheasant tail fibers with pearl Flashabou pulled over the top.

Frank Sawyer's famous Pheasant-Tail Nymph remains one of the top producers of trout. There are many variations of this pattern, a testament to its ability to catch fish; the Flashback Pheasant-Tail Nymph is one of these. The dash of flash on the back of the fly imitates the glossy appearance of the wing case on an emerging nymph. Try adding Flashabou wing cases to other nymph patterns; it's a cheap and easy way to improve these flies.

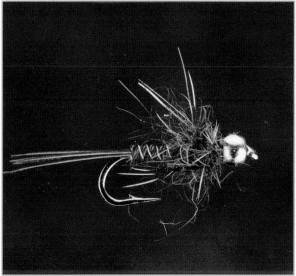

Hare E. Rooster

tied by Don Bastian
Cogan Station, Pennsylvania

Hook: 2X-long nymph hook, sizes 20 to 8.
Thread: Black, brown, tan, or olive 6/0.
Tail: Pheasant tail fibers.
Abdomen: Brown squirrel dubbing.
Rib: Extra fine gold wire.
Thorax: Gray squirrel dubbing.

Don ties his Hare E. Rooster in a variety of colors: brown, tan, olive, black, rust, and natural gray. The abdomen is very trim, but pick out the thorax with a bodkin. This is a simple, effective attractor pattern that does a fine job of imitating a wide variety of mayfly nymphs.

Don recommends fishing the Hare E. Rooster with a dead-drift retrieve, and occasionally allowing the fly to rise at the end of the swing. He typically uses a 4- to 6-weight rod.

Bead-head Hare E. Rooster

tied by Don Bastian
Cogan Station, Pennsylvania

Hook: 2X-long nymph hook, sizes 20 to 8.
Thread: Black, brown, tan, or olive 6/0.
Head: Small gold bead.
Tail: Pheasant tail fibers.
Abdomen: Brown squirrel dubbing.
Rib: Extra-fine gold wire.
Thorax: Gray squirrel dubbing.

This is the cousin to the standard Hare E. Rooster. Don Bastian says that this bead-headed version is actually better than the original pattern tied without the bead. Try the Bead-head Hare E. Rooster for fishing deep; switch to the beadless fly as the hatch progresses and the trout are feeding on the emergers.

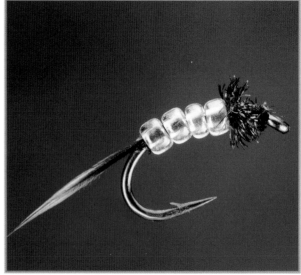

Latex Caddis Larva

tied by Don Bastian
Cogan Station, Pennsylvania

Hook: Bent-shank scud hook, sizes 20 and 18.
Thread: Olive or gray 6/0 or 8/0.
Abdomen: Brown, gray, green, olive, and black.
Thorax: Dark hare's-ear dubbing.

Don doesn't take credit for devising this pattern; he says Poul Jorgensen might have invented it. Don learned about it, however, from Rick Whorwood, of Stoney Creek, Ontario. Today, many tiers dress similar flies, and there are several synthetic materials on the market that can be used to tie segmented, realistic looking abdomens.

Pete's Eliminator

tied by Peter J. Bauer
Gardnerville, Nevada

Hook: Tiemco TMC2457, sizes 18 and 16.
Thread: Black 8/0.
Tail: Grizzly hackle fibers.
Abdomen: Four pink-pearl glass beads.
Thorax: Peacock herl.

Peter, who specializes in fishing Nevada's High Sierra lakes, fishes his Eliminator dead-drift behind an attractor dry fly. The idea of using small glass beads to make the body is very interesting. Crafts stores stock beads of almost every color and size, including some great looking peacock colored beads. You can use these to tie some excellent looking caddis larvae patterns. Glass beads are surprisingly durable, and give the fly a segmented appearance and nice fish-attracting glow.

Mac's Rock Worm

tied by Mac McGee
Chattanooga, Tennessee

Mac McGee has been a fly fisherman for twenty years, a guide for ten years, and has owned Choo Choo Fly & Tackle, a shop in Chattanooga, for the past two years. He specializes in fishing east Tennessee's fabulous tailwaters and mountain streams. This region of the country is a real sleeper when it comes to fine trout fishing; it has miles of excellent streams and a long season. You can fish the Great Smoky Mountains National Park or the Cherokee National Forest, as well as the rivers flowing below the dams operated by the Tennessee Valley Authority. And you have opportunities to catch brook, rainbow, and some monster brown trout.

Mac's Rock Worm is a good imitation of the caddis larvae that are common to these Southern streams and much of the United States. Mac says that this pattern is a "slight variation of others I have seen, but don't know who 'owns' it." He fishes this fly with a dead-drift retrieve with a 4- to 6-weight rod.

Hook: Bent-shank scud hook, size 12.
Thread: Black 6/0.
Head: Brass bead.
Abdomen: Olive Jelly Rope (Vinyl Rib is a good substitute).
Thorax: Peacock herl.

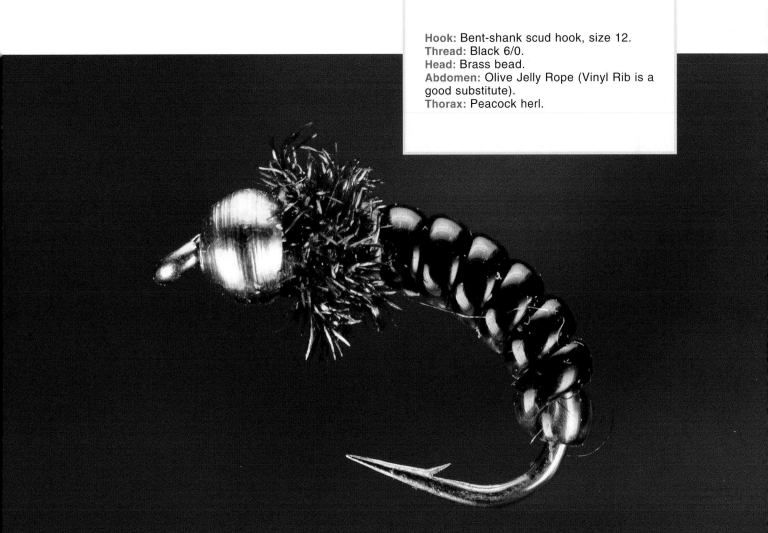

Hook: Tiemco TMC5262, sizes 14 to 10.
Thread: Brown 6/0.
Tail: Brown marabou.
Abdomen: Brown Kaufman Stonefly Blend dubbing.
Rib: Fine copper wire.
Thorax: Brown Kaufman Stonefly Blend dubbing.
Legs: Brown-and-orange flake Sili Legs.

The Superior X-Legs

tied by Matt Paulson
Superior, Wisconsin

Matt Paulson and Jeff Dahl operate a fly shop called The Superior Fly Angler. In their area they specialize in fishing for steelhead in the spring and fall, and smallmouth bass throughout the summer.

Paulson says that The Superior X-Legs is a generic imitation, but might possibly represent a stonefly nymph. He also says that "when steelheading, we generally fish the fly deep and use a strike indicator—pretty basic. Sometimes we fish it in tandem with an egg fly. Try different hand-retrieve speeds, and match your rod to the quarry. A seven- to eight-weight usually works fine."

Super Pupa

tied by Mary Kuss
Media, Pennsylvania

Mary Kuss has been fly fishing for thirty-five years, and has been guiding for twenty-two. Mary guides out of The Sporting Gentleman, a fly shop in Media, Pennsylvania.

Mary found this trout pattern in a British fly-fishing magazine. She says it's an imitation of a caddis emerger, and considers it a "go-to" fly in May and June when other patterns fail. Mary fishes the Super Pupa in the surface film at the end of a long 6X leader.

Hook: Regular dry-fly hook, sizes 18 to 14.
Thread: Brown 6/0 or 8/0.
Body: Olive dubbing.
Head: Dark brown dubbing.
Hackle: Brown, clipped on the top and bottom.

Hook: Regular wet-fly hook, sizes 18 to 12.
Thread: Black 6/0.
Body: Pearl Flashabou.
Hackle: Partridge.

Firehole Soft Hackle

tied by Dusty Wissmath
Raven Rocks, Virginia

Here's what Dusty Wissmath has to say about this delicate wet fly:

"The Firehole Soft Hackle is a fly that I came up with in the early eighties when I lived in Jackson, Wyoming. I was working at a fly shop and guiding on the Snake River and in Yellowstone National Park. Having just read one of Sylvester Nemes's books about soft hackles, I was enamored with the traditional soft hackles and updated the patterns by wrapping Flashabou over the thread body. As I form the thread body, I build up a small hump behind where the partridge hackle will be added. This takes the place of the dubbing. I then tie in and wrap a piece of Flashabou. I also coat the body with epoxy to make it more durable."

Dusty says that his Firehole Soft Hackle works great during a caddisfly hatch to imitate the emerging insects. He likes to fish it using the old "Leisenring Lift," which raises the fly up in the water column like it's an insect struggling to the surface. He has tied the fly using different colors of Flashabou, but says that pearl catches more fish. Dusty says that the pearl probably does a better job of imitating the bright gas bubbles that form under the skin of the emerging insect.

In addition to guiding on Virginia's mountain streams for native brook trout, he also operates a fly-fishing school that helps anglers improve their skills. Dusty offers a one-day Basic Casting Clinic, a one-day Advanced Casting Techniques Clinic, and a two-day Introduction to Fly Fishing.

Chip's Gitter

tied by Reg "Chip" Chipman
Nutrioso, Arizona

Hook: Orvis 8891 or Tiemco TMC2457, size 14.
Thread: Dark brown 6/0.
Bead: ⅛-inch diameter gold bead.
Body: Dark brown, green, or your choice of dubbing.
Rib: Fine gold dubbing.

Chip Chipman has been fly fishing for forty-eight years, and guiding the past four. Chip fishes the White Mountains of Arizona for Apache, brown, and rainbow trout.

His fly, Chip's Gitter, is a good general imitation of a caddis pupa. Chip says this pattern "is very generic. I use brown because so many insects in various developmental stages are brown, and there are a lot of *Brachycentrus americanus* in our stream, so the green works well."

In addition to using these Gitters on his home waters in Arizona, Chip has also used these flies successfully in Utah, Wyoming, and Wisconsin. Tie Chip's Gitter in body colors to match the naturals in your local stream or pond.

Killer Emerger

tied by Bob Mallard
Madison, Maine

Hook: Tiemco TMC2487, sizes 14 and 12.
Thread: Dark brown 8/0.
Trailing shuck: Olive Antron.
Abdomen: Fine brown dubbing.
Thorax: Hendrickson pink dubbing.
Head: Peacock dubbing.
Wing: Brown partridge fibers and two strands of ultra-violet pearl Krystal Flash.
Bead: Small pearl bead.

Bob Mallard owns a beautiful shop in Madison, Maine. It's a first-rate outfit that carries everything you'll need for fishing in Maine.

Bob uses his Killer Emerger to match a wide variety of hatching mayflies and caddisflies on the Kennebec River and other local waters. He fishes the Killer Emerger down and across, just under the surface.

You'll notice the glass bead for the head. This bead gives the front of the fly a bright glow, similar to the gas generated in the skin of an emerging pupa or nymph. Spirit River markets these tiny beads for tying flies, but you can also find small beads in many craft stores.

Marabou Foam Emerger

tied by Tony Mastaler
Springfield, Vermont

Hook: Long-shank dry-fly hook, sizes 14 and 12.
Thread: Black 6/0.
Tail: Fine black marabou fibers.
Abdomen: Fine black dubbing.
Rib: Fine silver wire.
Thorax: Black marabou placed in a dubbing loop.
Post: Black closed-cell foam.
Wing case: Peacock herl, separated and pulled around the foam post.
Legs: Brown speckled hen hackle.

Tony Mastaler ties the Marabou Foam Emerger in a variety of colors to match his local hatches, and you can, too. Olive, light olive, brown, and tan are all good colors. He prefers fishing this pattern with a 5-weight outfit and a 10- to 12-foot-long, 4X to 6X leader.

In addition to guiding, Tony ties flies for shops and anglers. While he specializes in patterns that catch fish on his local waters, he has dressed flies for fishing in Iceland, New Zealand, and Argentina.

Kashner Caddis Pupa

tied by Chuck Kashner
Pawlet, Vermont

Today there's a mad dash to use synthetic materials to tie caddis pupae. Kashner's Caddis Pupa is made entirely out of natural ingredients. While caddis pupae imitations are not the most handsome flies, Chuck Kashner's pattern is well tied and will obviously catch fish.

Gary LaFontaine, in his important book *Caddisflies*, recommends fishing a pupa imitation when you see trout swirling under the surface but not feeding on the top. I've followed his suggestion and it works. Cast the fly down-and-across stream, allow it to sink a few inches, and then use a retrieve with short strips to mimic a caddis pupa struggling to the surface.

Hook: Mustad 3906, sizes 16 to 8.
Thread: Brown or olive 6/0.
Body: Light tan, dark tan, or olive hare's-ear dubbing.
Rib: Gold or copper wire.
Antennae: Wood-duck flank fibers.
Wing: Pheasant or duck wing quill segments.
Legs: Hen pheasant or grouse fibers.
Head: Dark brown dubbing.

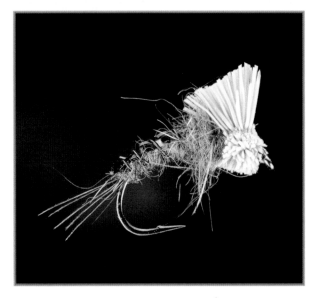

Hatching Nymph

tied by Thomas Baltz
Mt. Holly Springs, Pennsylvania

Hook: Daiichi 1130, sizes 18 to 12.
Thread: Olive 6/0.
Tail: Pheasant tail fibers.
Abdomen: Hare's mask dubbing.
Back: Dark bronze Flashabou.
Rib: Copper wire.
Thorax: Hare's mask dubbing.
Head: Natural deer hair, spun and clipped short to leave an emerging wing.

This is another pattern that can be tied in colors to imitate your local mayflies: olive, tan, brown, pale yellow, and even white to match the famous white-fly hatch. Pick a few fibers out of the thorax to imitate legs.

"Use fly floatant on the deer-hair head and even the tippet to suspend the nymph at the surface," says Baltz. "This is a generic pattern that I came up with to suggest any number of different mayfly nymphs in the emerging process, and is a killer on flat water. The color of the design may be adjusted to create patterns to match specific species. One version, which has become a local favorite, is tied for use during the white-fly hatch on the Yellow Breeches."

Brown Pupa

tied by Robert Lewis
Pound Ridge, New York

Hook: Curved-shank nymph hook, sizes 16 to 12.
Thread: Dark brown 6/0.
Body: Nymph Skin colored with a brown permanent marker.
Legs: Emu dyed brown.
Wing case: Thin Skin colored with a dark brown permanent marker.
Head: Small black bead.

I first met Robert Lewis at a fly-fishing show in Marlboro, Massachusetts. He was with a mutual friend who was also a guide. Robert showed me some of his flies, and it was obvious that he is a talented tier. This Brown Pupa is a good example of his work.

Thin Skin, which is used to tie the body of the Brown Pupa, is imported from England, and can be found at a growing number of fly shops. It is a latex, rubberband sort of material that makes great-looking larvae bodies. You can color Thin Skin with permanent markers.

The emu feather, used to tie the legs of the Brown Pupa, is sort of a jumbo marabou fiber. The emu gives the fly life when it is fished.

Sulphur Middle Man

tied by Justin Moeykens
New Boston, New Hampshire

Hook: Tiemco TMC200R, sizes 18 and 16.
Thread: Orange 6/0.
Trailing shuck: Light dun Darlon.
Abdomen: Sulphur turkey biot.
Thorax: Sulphur beaver dubbing.
Wing case: Light dun Darlon.
Legs: Lemon wood duck.

Sulphur mayflies are widespread across North America, offering some of the best and most reliable fishing of the season. The Sulphur Middle Man is a good imitation of a sulphur emerger; it is especially productive early in the hatch. Fish the pattern upstream on a leader greased with floatant.

BWO Middle Man

tied by Justin Moeykens
New Boston, New Hampshire

Hook: Tiemco TMC200R, sizes 20 to 16.
Thread: Dark olive 6/0.
Trailing shuck: Olive Darlon.
Abdomen: Turkey biot dyed the color of a blue-winged olive.
Thorax: Blue-winged olive beaver dubbing.
Wing case: Light dun Darlon.
Legs: Lemon wood duck.

The BWO Middle Man works throughout the season to match blue-winged olive emergers. Like its cousin, the Sulphur Middle Man, this pattern works best early in the hatch. It is a small, delicate fly, and is fun to use with the lightest tackle. Fish the BWO Middle Man with a dead-drift presentation and a leader greased with fly floatant.

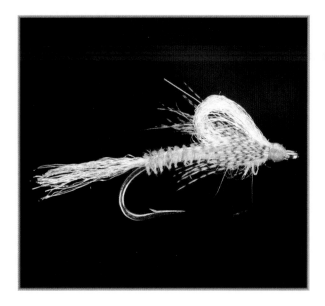

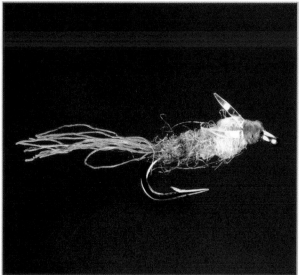

PMD Middle Man

tied by Justin Moeykens
New Boston, New Hampshire

Hook: Tiemco TMC200R, sizes 20 to 16.
Thread: Gray 6/0.
Trailing shuck: Light dun Darlon.
Abdomen: Turkey biot dyed the color of a pale morning dun.
Thorax: Pale morning dun beaver dubbing.
Wing case: Light dun Darlon.
Legs: Lemon wood duck.

The PMD Middle Man is another of Justin Moeykens's original series of emerger patterns. Fish the PMD Middle Man whenever you encounter a hatch of pale morning duns. Fish the fly early in the hatch when the insects are just beginning to pop onto the surface. This pattern works best fished with a dead-drift presentation.

Krystal Emerger

tied by Rick Murphy
Colorado Springs, Colorado

Hook: Tiemco TMC100, sizes 24 to 20.
Thread: Gray 8/0.
Trailing shuck: Rust Antron.
Abdomen: Olive brown Superfine dubbing.
Thorax: Cream Superfine dubbing.
Wing case: Pearl Krystal Flash.

I use this pattern all season long to match midges and blue-winged olives," says Rick Murphy.

With respect to tying the Krystal Emerger, he offered the following tip for making the wing case:

"I pull the Krystal Flash forward over the top, and then fold it down the sides to form the legs. I then trim the legs slightly longer than the wing case."

Caddis Emerger

tied by Rick Murphy
Colorado Springs, Colorado

This is a copy of Gary LaFontaine's famous pattern called the Sparkle Caddis Emerger. It's a great fly that catches trout all over the country. Rick Murphy likes to fish the Caddis Emerger behind a caddis dry fly. In addition, he ties a bead-head version of the Caddis Emerger for fishing deep.

Hook: Tiemco TMC100, sizes 18 and 16.
Thread: Rust 8/0.
Trailing shuck & veil: Rust Antron.
Underbody: Rust tying thread.
Legs: Partridge fibers.
Head: Peacock herl.

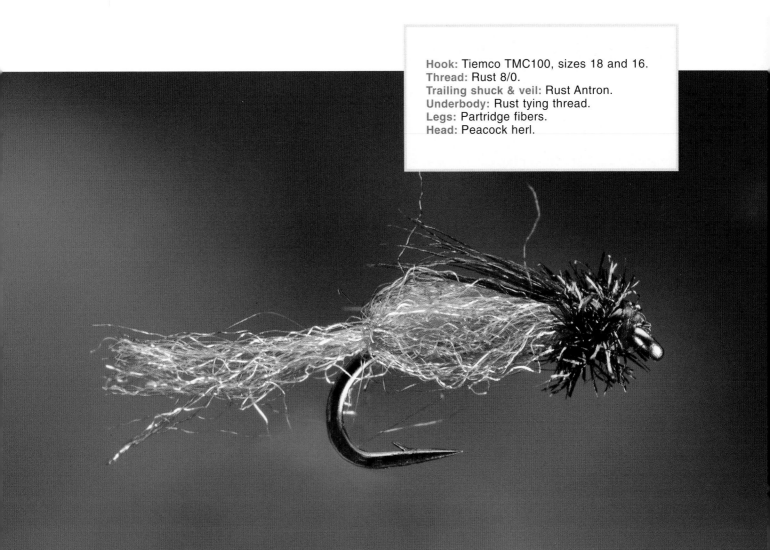

Hook: Daiichi 1100, size to match the natural.
Thread: Olive 6/0.
Tails: Dark dun Microfibbetts.
Wing: Cream Hi-Viz.
Body: Olive rabbit dubbing.
Hackle: Grizzly dyed olive.

I.C.S.I. (I Can See It) Blue-Wing Olive

tied by Thomas Baltz
Mt. Holly Springs, Pennsylvania

Here's another example of a tiny parachute dry fly; in this case, tied on a size 22 hook. It takes remarkable skill to tie such a small parachute. Creating too much bulk on the hook is one of the chief enemies to tying a dainty small fly. To reduce the bulk, Tom Baltz uses synthetic Hi-Viz for the wing post; a lot of tiers use deer hair for the wing post, but this creates too much bulk on the hook shank. Tom ties a piece of Hi-Viz under the hook to look like splayed spent-spinner wings; he uses two or three figure-eight wraps to secure the material in place. Next, Tom pulls the wings up, and makes two or three "gathering" wraps around the base of the wing post on top of the hook shank. This method creates a durable wing that adds almost no bulk to the fly. The Hi-Viz wing (you may substitute with polypropylene yarn) is also easy to see on the water, a great feature when fishing a small fly under low-light conditions.

"As far as I know, George Harvey, of State College, Pennsylvania, was the first to use brightly colored wings," says Tom Baltz. "I resisted this idea for many years—for aesthetic reasons—but finally gave it a try on my Para Nymph pattern. My clients were having plenty of trout take their flies, but were late in striking because of the difficulty of seeing these small, dark flies on the water. With the bright wing, the fly is much easier to keep an eye on and the trout do not seem to care at all. These bright wings have been extensively tested on the hard-fished waters of the Yellow Breeches and Letort, among other streams."

Ron's Midge

tied by Ron Kozlowski
Nickolson, Pennsylvania

Hook: Bent-shank light-wire hook, sizes 22 and 20.
Thread: Black 14/0.
Body: Tying thread.
Wing post: Orange Antron yarn.
Hackle: Grizzly.

This might be the smallest fly submitted to this project. And best of all, it's beautifully tied. Dressing small parachute patterns is tough enough, but Ron Kozlowski really pushed the limit with this example. This fly would be perfect for matching a hatch of the smallest midges, and test the tying skills of the most ardent dry-fly aficionado.

Kashner Midge

tied by Chuck Kashner
Pawlet, Vermont

Hook: Mustad 94840, sizes 24 to 16.
Thread: Black 8/0.
Abdomen: Tying thread.
Thorax: Black dry-fly dubbing.
Wing post: 12-pound-test monofilament.
Hackle: Grizzly.

This basic parachute midge lies low against the water surface. The Kashner Midge proves that you can tie a very effective fly using only a couple of materials.

Several guides submitted parachute patterns for this book. A parachute hackle creates a very realistic "footprint" on the water, and the body of the fly is slung low against the surface. When tied well, these flies are surprisingly durable.

Some tiers prefer using polypropylene yarn for the post around which they wrap the hackle; they leave the yarn a little long to create the wing of the fly. Chuck Kashner, however, used monofilament for the hackle post, and clipped the mono short after wrapping the feather. He also applied a drop of cement to the post to help secure the hackle in place.

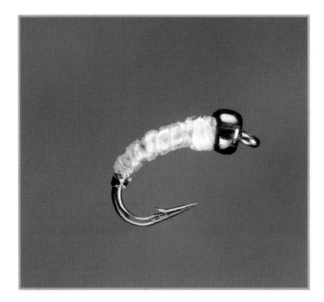

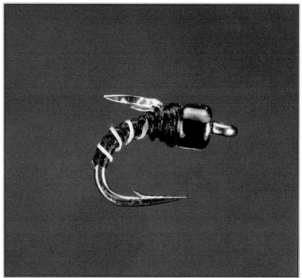

U.V. Midge

tied by Rick Murphy
Colorado Springs, Colorado

Hook: Tiemco TMC2487, sizes 22 and 20.
Thread: White 8/0.
Head: Extra small root-beer bead.
Body: Ultraviolet Krystal Flash and clear Micro Tubing.

Some anglers specialize in tying and fishing really tiny flies. Rick Murphy fishes waters that would challenge the most diehard midge aficionado; Colorado's South Platte River is famous for the demands it places on the technical fly fisherman.

Rick fishes the U.V. Midge as the dropper on a tandem rig. This pattern is little but bright, and stands out in clear water. There are times when surprisingly large trout feed on small midges. Rick ties the U.V. Midge to catch rainbow, brown, and cutthroat trout, especially throughout the winter. And best of all, he uses lightweight gear: a 4-weight rod and a 6X fluorocarbon leader.

Black & Peacock Midge

tied by Rick Murphy
Colorado Springs, Colorado

Hook: Tiemco TMC2487, sizes 22 and 20.
Thread: Black 8/0.
Head: Extra-small peacock-green bead.
Body: Tying thread.
Rib: White FisHair or fine silver wire.
Wing: Pearl Krystal Flash.

Guide Rick Murphy uses the Black & Peacock as a dropper on a tandem-fly rig. This fly will work wherever trout feed on extra-small midges.

I.C.S.I. (I Can See It) Midge

tied by Thomas Baltz
Mt. Holly Springs, Pennsylvania

And the flies just keep getting smaller!

Tom Baltz uses a variety of materials to tie this pattern to match different midges. He substitutes the color of thread to match the body. And he often swaps the muskrat dubbing for rabbit dubbing, peacock quill, or Flashabou. Tom says that this fly can also be used to match small species of mayflies.

"I first tied this pattern to fish during the blue-winged olive hatches for when the fish are reluctant to take surface flies. I incorporated the orange wing post so my clients could see it on the water. Over time, I've gotten comfortable with the bright wing. It has proven very effective during a variety of 'sipping' situations on flat water. Orvis sells this pattern, and it's done well all over the country.

"When fishing the fly, use a 6X or 7X tippet, and grease only the hackle. Use your fingernail to spread the wing post; this will make the 'spot' appear larger and easier to see."

Hook: Daiichi 1100, sizes 24 to 18.
Thread: Olive 6/0.
Body: Muskrat belly fur.
Wing post: Calftail, dyed hot orange.
Hackle: Grizzly.

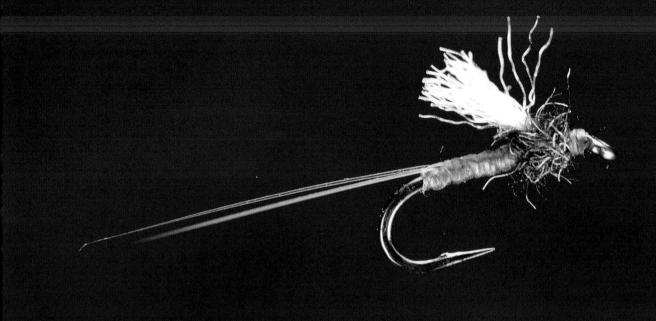

Hook: Tiemco TMC100, sizes 24 to 20.
Thread: Size 8/0, color to match the thorax.
Tail: Light dun Microfibbetts.
Abdomen: Tying thread.
Thorax: Superfine dubbing.
Wing: White SAAP Body Fur.

RS 2

tied by Rick Murphy
Colorado Springs, Colorado

According to guide Rick Murphy, "I tie this fly, which was developed by Rim Chung, in gray, olive and black. We use this fly all year to match midges, blue-winged olives, pale morning duns and Tricos. Dead-drift it along the bottom behind an attractor or larger nymph, or use it behind a parachute dry fly with about twenty-four inches of fluorocarbon."

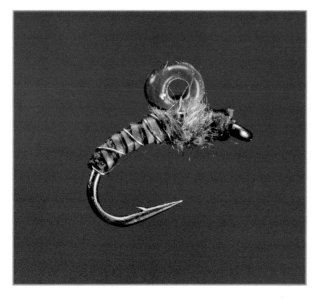 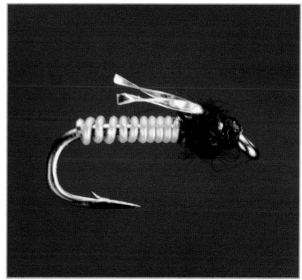

Bubble Midge

tied by Rick Murphy
Colorado Springs, Colorado

Hook: Tiemco TMC2487, sizes 22 and 20.
Thread: Gray 8/0.
Bubble: Extra-small silver glass bead.
Abdomen: Stripped peacock herl.
Rib: Extra fine silver wire.
Thorax: Superfine olive brown dubbing.

"I use this fly from October through May," says Rick Murphy. "I dead-drift it along the bottom behind a Bead-head attractor pattern. I prefer to use a nine-foot-long, four-weight rod."

Murphy begins the Bubble Midge by tying the tiny glass bead on top of the hook shank. This bead, which has a faint glow, represents the air sack of an emerging midge. The company Spirit River distributes these small glass beads; look for them in your local fly shop. Many crafts stores also stock small glass beads; these usually aren't as tiny as the Spirit River product, but they come in a wide variety of colors and are excellent for tying small and medium-sized nymphs and midge larvae.

South Platte Brassie

tied by Rick Murphy
Colorado Springs, Colorado

Hook: Tiemco TMC100, sizes 26 to 20.
Thread: Black 8/0.
Body: Copper, chartreuse, or red wire.
Wing: Pearl Krystal Flash.
Head: Black thread or Superfine dubbing.

The South Platte Brassie was one of the first patterns tied with a wire body. The wire adds weight to the fly and allows it to quickly sink. Although it was designed for fishing Colorado's South Platte River, the South Platte Brassie works on most streams where the trout key in on small midges. Wapsi Fly's narrow-diameter Ultra Wire comes in almost two dozen colors, allowing you to tie Brassies that match almost any midge.

Hook: Long-shank streamer hook, sizes 4 and 2.
Thread: Size 6/0, color to match the body.
Head & body: Dyed rabbit strip.

Leather-Head Sculpin

tied by Rob McLean
Rawlins, Wyoming

Rob McLean, owner of Freestone Flies & Guide Service, has developed a unique method of dyeing variegated bars on rabbit pelts, marabou, deer hair, and other materials. After dyeing the rabbit pelts, he cuts them into thin Zonker strips that can be used to create very realistic baitfish patterns, such as the Leather-Head Sculpin.

Begin the Leather-Head Sculpin by tying a short piece of rabbit strip to each side of the hook to form the pectoral fins of the baitfish. Next, clip the strips to match the shape of a real sculpin; Rob McLean places each strip on a template to help clip the leather. Tie these strips behind the hook eye, and then glue the two together.

Select rabbit strips in colors to match the baitfish in your local waters. This fly will work wherever big trout feed on sculpins. Rob McLean recommends fishing the Leather-Head Sculpin with a 6- to 8-weight rod. He prefers a full-sinking line for fishing deep, fast runs, and uses a floating line when casting into shallow water.

Modern Pheasant Salmon Fly

tied by Deborah Duran
Taunton, Massachusetts

Here's a modern interpretation of an Atlantic salmon fly. This pattern has a unique look and is beautifully executed.

Hook: Partridge Traditional Bartleet Supreme, size 1/0.
Thread: Black Flat-Waxed Nylon.
Tag: Small oval silver tinsel.
Body: Black Bill's Bodi Braid.
Wing: Two strands of black holographic tinsel with two matched silver pheasant neck feathers with white horizontal stripes.
Topping: One silver pheasant crest and one golden pheasant crest dyed red.
Cheek: English Jay with wood duck covering the bottom half of the Jay feather, and jungle cock.
Throat: One folded silver pheasant feather.

Hook: Long-shank nymph hook, size 6.
Thread: Size 6/0, color to match the body.
Tail: Rabbit strip.
Collar: A piece of crosscut rabbit strip wrapped around the hook behind the eye.

Barred Leech

tied by Rob McLean
Rawlins, Wyoming

Nothing in nature is one solid color, and here we see how Rob McLean's uniquely dyed rabbit strips are used to tie realistic flies. The Barred Leech is simple to tie, and will catch trout and bass. This is one of McLean's favorite patterns for fishing in low-light conditions and at night. He fishes the Barred Leech along the bottom with a slow, methodical retrieve.

Kennebec Sculpin

tied by Bob Mallard
Madison, Maine

Hook: 4X-long streamer hook, size 4.
Thread: Black 6/0.
Tail: Olive variant Zonker strip.
Body: Lots of lead wire and pearl Lite Brite dubbing.
Collar: Red Lite Brite dubbing and olive rubber legs.
Back: Olive wool and peacock Krystal Flash.
Head: Olive wool.
Eyes: White and black paint.

I'm placing this sculpin imitation here with the rest of the trout patterns, but it is also a great bass fly. Bob Mallard uses the Kennebec Sculpin when he floats the Kennebec River; he bangs this fly up against the bank, uses a strip retrieve, and catches some very big trout.

Bead-head White Crystal Woolly Bugger

tied by Scott Sickau
Boone, Iowa

Hook: Daiichi 1710, sizes 16 to 12.
Thread: White 8/0.
Head: Silver tungsten bead, sized to match the hook.
Tail: White marabou and one strand of pearl Krystal Flash divided into eight equal pieces.
Body: White chenille.
Hackle: White 8/0.

Scott Sickau has fished central Iowa for over twenty-five years, and operates a fly-tying materials catalog outfit called Hatch's Fly Tying Supplies. Scott offers guided trips as well as tying and casting classes.

Sickau's Bead-head White Crystal Woolly Bugger is a simple but effective pattern for fishing in the early morning and late evening. He fishes the fly twelve to twenty-four inches below a foam strike indicator using a slow, steady stripping retrieve. This fly would catch trout as well as panfish.

Plattsburgh Spey

tied by William Stahl
Wilmington, New York

Hook: Atlantic-salmon hook, sizes 8 to 2.
Thread: Black 6/0.
Tag: Clear holographic tinsel.
Butt: Peacock herl.
Body: Pearl Diamond Braid.
Lower underwing: Pearl Flashabou.
Upper underwing: Black and pearl Krystal Flash.
Collar: Mallard flank feather, folded and wrapped around the hook shank, followed by a wood duck flank feather, also folded and wrapped around the hook.
Head: Black thread.
Eyes: Small adhesive eyes coated with epoxy.

Bill Stahl says that the Plattsburgh Spey does a good job at imitating a smelt; at least the landlocked salmon and trout take the fly when they are turned on to smelt.

Bill guides anglers to a variety of fishing: salmon, trout, bass, pike, and even muskie. He also does a considerable amount of duck hunting, all in the beautiful Adirondacks.

914

tied by Mac Huff
Joseph, Oregon

Hook: Orvis 122J bent-shank nymph hook, sizes 8 to 4.
Thread: Black 3/0.
Weight: Brass cone.
Body: White and black marabou.

Guide Mac Huff fishes northeast Oregon's and southwest Washington's lakes and rivers for trout, steelhead, and smallmouth bass. Mac is a wildlife biologist and Federation of Fly Fishers certified casting instructor.

The 914 is a simple, effective fly. There's a brass cone buried under all of that marabou. The rest of the fly is made of thread and marabou. You can easily alter the fly by changing the color of the marabou.

Huff says the 914 is a useful attractor pattern. He generally fishes it dead-drift with occasional twitches to bring the marabou to life. He uses it as a primary fly or a dropper.

The Bunkhouse

tied by William Stahl
Wilmington, New York

I first met Bill Stahl at Fran Better's Adirondack Sports, located along the Ausable River in the heart of the Adirondacks. I was representing *American Angler* and *Fly Tyer* magazines at the ESPN Great Outdoors Games. It was Saturday afternoon, and the contestants in the fly-fishing competition were on the river. Members of the media were barred from covering the actual competition—this was fine with me because I wasn't terribly interested in tagging along while others fished—and I stopped into the legendary fly shop to check on the local fishing conditions and meet Fran.

Bill was busy waiting on customers while Fran sat in a rocking chair and tied flies. We had a pleasant conversation, and Bill told me about his fledgling operation called The Bunkhouse. The Bunkhouse is a sort of an anglers retreat, a place to get away for a few days of low-key fishing. You might call it "family-style fly fishing."

Bill ties The Bunkhouse, which he uses to catch trout and smallmouth bass, to commemorate his anglers getaway.

Hook: Straight-eye streamer hook, sizes 8 to 4.
Thread: Dark olive 6/0.
Tail: Red hackle fibers.
Body: Dark olive thread.
Rib: Hot-orange copper wire and round silver tinsel.
Wing: Bucktail dyed orange.
Topping: Widgeon flank fibers.
Collar: Furnace hackle.

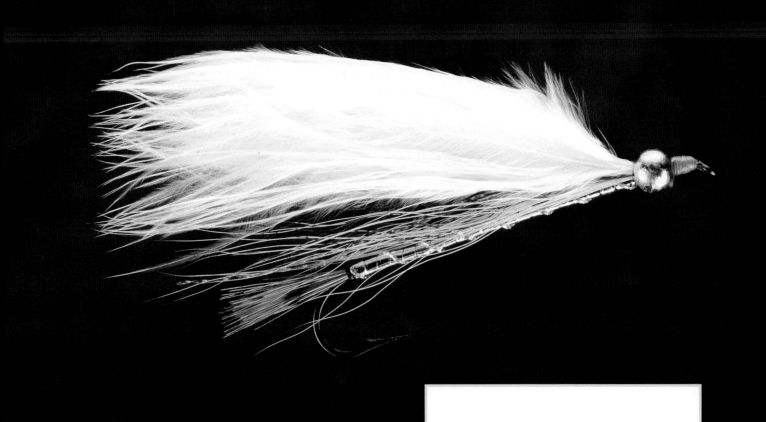

Hook: 6X- to 8X-long streamer hook,
sizes 6 to 2.
Thread: Orange or red 6/0.
Bead: Medium gold bead.
Tail: Golden-pheasant tippet fibers.
Body: Flat silver tinsel.
Rib: Narrow silver oval tinsel.
Underwing: Yellow bucktail, red bucktail,
and pearl Krystal Flash.
Wing: White marabou.

Bead-head Schufelt Special

tied by Ian Cameron
Glenburn, Maine

According to Ian Cameron, "Bobby Schufelt, of Greenville, Maine, lays claim to this fly. But let's be honest here: it is essentially a dressed-up Mickey Finn with a white marabou wing over the top. But this pattern does work well for landlocked salmon and brook trout."

That's the story about the Schufelt Special, now let me tell you a little bit about the Ian.

Ian is a longtime buddy of mine. He's a great friend and a superb guide. He specializes in fishing for landlocked salmon on Maine's West Branch of the Penobscot River (many consider this the premier landlocked-salmon river in the United States), and the East Outlet of the Kennebec River. Ian and I have spent dozens of hours fishing together, and I always have a wonderful time. He runs a drift boat down these major rivers, and we've always caught fish. Best of all, Ian is a pleasure to be with; he's very intelligent and witty, and there's never a dull moment.

If you're interested at a shot at a big Maine landlocked salmon, give Ian Cameron a call.

Bleeding Black Ghost Marabou Modified

tied by Ian Cameron
Glenburn, Maine

Guide Ian Cameron tells the story of his Bleeding Black Ghost Marabou Modified:

"Herbert Welch first tied this fly in nineteen twenty-six at Haines Landing on Mooselookmeguntic Lake, Maine. The original was a feather-wing streamer tied in the classic Maine style, like the Gray Ghost. I feel that the marabou wing adds more movement. And, because I like to sink flies, I have added a tungsten cone head. Further modifications include pearl Flashabou and a red hackle throat over the yellow hackle throat. This theoretically represents gills or a 'bleeding' throat. Because the Black Ghost is an 'upside down' streamer—it has a dark body and a light top—I have put peacock herl over the white wing to help balance its silhouette."

Ian brings up an interesting point about the Black Ghost. This pattern is supposed to be a loose imitation of a baitfish, but a real baitfish has a light colored belly and a darker back. However, the Black Ghost remains a top fish-catcher. Over the years, though, Ian has tied progressively smaller streamers. "While I am a firm believer in 'big flies, big fish,' I am beginning to think that perhaps a smaller streamer is more effective. Another technique that works is to tie on a smaller attractor as a dropper behind a Woolly Bugger. This seems to stimulate the fish into striking. Maybe it looks like a minnow getting some food that the big guys are missing."

Hook: 6X- to 8X-long streamer hook, sizes 6 to 2.
Thread: Black 6/0.
Head: Medium tungsten cone or bead.
Tail: Yellow hackle fibers.
Body: Black floss, wool yarn, or chenille.
Throat: Yellow and red hackle fibers.
Wing: Strands of pearl Flashabou and black marabou.
Topping: Six strands of peacock herl.

Gray Ghost Marabou

tied by Ian Cameron
Glenburn, Maine

Hook: 6X- to 8X-long streamer hook, sizes 6 to 2.
Thread: Black 6/0 with the characteristic Carrie Stevens stripe in the middle of the head.
Tag: Flat silver tinsel.
Body: Orange floss.
Rib: Flat silver tinsel.
Throat: White bucktail and a short golden-pheasant crest feather.
Underwing: A golden-pheasant crest feather equal to the length of the hook shank and curving down, and four to six strands of peacock herl.
Wing: Gray marabou.
Shoulders: Silver pheasant body feathers.

Some patterns reach legendary status within our sport. Years ago, the U.S. Postal Service came up with their list of important flies and put them on postage stamps: the Royal Wulff, Stu Apte's Tarpon Fly, Muddler Minnow, and Lefty's Deceiver. These are all great patterns that have wide appeal, but it's too bad they didn't include the Gray Ghost. The Gray Ghost is an old classic pattern that any experienced fly fisher will recognize. When it is tied well, it is extremely beautiful. And, of course, a woman developed it; the Postal department's list was decidedly chauvinistic.

Ian Cameron is partial to streamers tied with marabou wings. Marabou seems like a frail material, but it is very durable. When a fish strikes a fly sporting a marabou wing, the soft fibers are gently pushed to the side. And no material—natural or synthetic—duplicates the breathing, pulsating qualities of marabou. It really is one of the most important fly-tying materials.

In addition to being one of Maine's leading landlocked-salmon guides, Ian Cameron is also the director of program operations for River Therapy, a service dedicated to improving relationships within couples and families. River Therapy is unique service helping couples, families, and other groups improve communication.

Super Muddler

tied by Robert Lewis
Pound Ridge, New York

Hook: Tiemco TMC9395, sizes 8 to 2.
Thread: White Monocord.
Body: Pearl Estaz.
Tail: A strip of pine squirrel dyed olive.
Rib: Clear monofilament.
Pectoral fins: Hungarian partridge body feathers.
Gills: Red Crystal Chenille.
Head: Black deer hair, spun and clipped to shape.

"On the Delaware River, night fishing with big Muddler and sculpin patterns can yield great results," says Rob Lewis. His Super Muddler will work wherever sculpin are a part of the trouts's diets.

Note the loop of 25-pound-test monofilament at the end of the hook shank. This loop keeps the wing from fouling around the hook. This is a good idea that can be used on a large number of flies.

Feel free to substitute a rabbit strip for the squirrel. Some fly shops carry squirrel strips, but this material can be a little tough to find; almost all fly shops stock rabbit Zonker strips.

The Golden Angel

tied by Justin Moeykens
New Boston, New Hampshire

Hook: Partridge SEB, sizes 10 to 4.
Thread: Hot Orange 8/0.
Tag: Flat gold tinsel.
Tail: Hot orange Schlappen.
Body: Lemon yellow floss.
Rib: Flat gold tinsel.
Wing: Lemon wood duck.
Collar: Hot orange saddle hackle.

This streamer is a good choice for fishing in spring and fall. According to guide Justin Moeykens, the Golden Angel was "originated for fall landlocked salmon, however, I've found that this fly also works for spring landlocks as well. I find that this fly fishes best in lower light scenarios such as evening and early morning."

The Golden Angel is a general attractor pattern. Fish it down-and-across stream.

Hook: Tiemco TMC8089, sizes 10 to 2.
Thread: Tan Danville Flymaster Plus.
Weed guard: 25-pound-test monofilament.
Tail: Tan rabbit strip.
Body: Tan crosscut rabbit strip.
Collar: Natural deer hair.
Head: Natural deer hair.

Stanley Waker Maker

tied by Justin Moeykens
New Boston, New Hampshire

According to Justin Moeykens, "This pattern was developed by Steve Stanley to appear as a wounded fish coming out of a dam spillway. It should be fished just below the surface with a slack line. The rabbit strip provides its own motion. On still water, the fly should be fished just below the surface with long strips followed by short pauses."

The Stanley Waker Maker catches trout, landlocked salmon, bass, and pike.

Tying flies to imitate wounded baitfish isn't as outlandish as it sounds. On the West Branch of the Penobscot River, the country's leading producer of big landlocked salmon, anglers use a pattern called the West Branch Dry Fly. This pattern is nothing more than a piece of round closed-cell foam inserted into a 3- to 4-inch-long length of EZ-Body Tubing. A hook is inserted in one end of the tubing, and both ends are closed tight with thread. Some tiers epoxy a single eye on the bottom of the fly; the fly looks like a dying fish lying on its side. The West Branch Dry Fly is used to imitate a smelt that gets blown through the turbines on Ripogenous Dam at the head of the best section of the river. I've used this pattern to catch salmon measuring up to 22 inches long.

I suspect there are many instances on tailwaters where the largest fish feed on baitfish that get wounded coming through the dams. We're so concerned, however, with trying to match the hatch, that we overlook these unique opportunities.

Kate's Fancy

tied by Justin Moeykens
New Boston, New Hampshire

Hook: Partridge SEB, sizes 10 to 4.
Thread: Red 8/0.
Tag: Flat silver tinsel.
Tail: Red Schlappen.
Body: Gray Ghost orange floss.
Rib: Flat silver tinsel.
Wing: Lemon wood duck.
Collar: Red saddle hackle.

Justin Moeykens designed Kate's Fancy as a companion to Greg Nault's Golden Angel. This pattern also fishes best in the morning and early evening during spring and fall. And just like the Golden Angel, Justin fishes Kate's Fancy down-and-across stream.

Whoa Nellie

tied by Garret Booth
Temple, New Hampshire

Hook: Partridge Carrie Stevens streamer hook, size 4.
Thread: Black 8/0.
Tag: Oval silver tinsel.
Body: Lavender floss.
Rib: Oval silver tinsel.
Throat: Pink saddle hackle fibers with white hackle fibers on the bottom.
Wing: Four white saddle hackles.
Topping: Strands of lavender Krystal Flash and six peacock herls.

This fly was created by my wife, Nellie, in an effort to imitate the smelt photographs I came home with one afternoon after finding a few of the baitfish floating on the surface of Lake Winnipesaukee," says Garret. "Tied in this manner (on a long-shank hook), it is customarily trolled. Other variations of this pattern for casting are tied on a shorter shank hooks. We look forward to casting this fly in the spring to mix things up."

Use the Whoa Nellie in the spring after ice-out to catch landlocked salmon and trout.

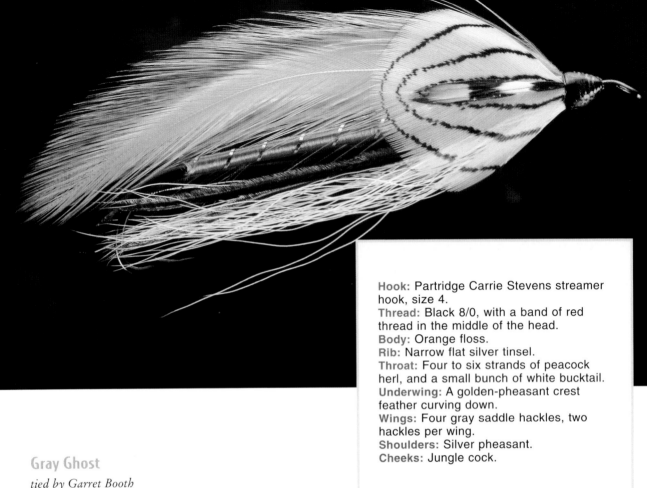

Hook: Partridge Carrie Stevens streamer hook, size 4.
Thread: Black 8/0, with a band of red thread in the middle of the head.
Body: Orange floss.
Rib: Narrow flat silver tinsel.
Throat: Four to six strands of peacock herl, and a small bunch of white bucktail.
Underwing: A golden-pheasant crest feather curving down.
Wings: Four gray saddle hackles, two hackles per wing.
Shoulders: Silver pheasant.
Cheeks: Jungle cock.

Gray Ghost

tied by Garret Booth
Temple, New Hampshire

Alright, there's nothing new about the Gray Ghost. So what? It's still one of the most beautiful patterns ever created, and Garret Booth dressed a lovely rendition.

Maine legend Carrie Stevens first tied the Gray Ghost in the 1930s. This pattern quickly became famous for catching big landlocked salmon and brook trout, and it is now considered a true classic. Tiers throughout the Northeast still dress the Gray Ghost for fishing as well as framing.

Let me share a couple of observations about the Gray Ghost. First, I continue to see the name of the fly spelled in two different ways: Grey Ghost, and Gray Ghost. What's the difference? "Grey" is the English spelling; "gray" is the American. Carrie Stevens spelled it Gray Ghost, and I do, too. Aside from taking her lead in the spelling of the name of the fly, I don't see anything wrong with altering the dressing. Garret Booth, for instance, ties a slightly stripped-down version of the pattern; his fly lacks a silver tinsel tag and golden-pheasant crest belly. These are very minor alterations that will have no impact on the fly's ability to catch fish.

Just in case you're not familiar with the Gray Ghost, Garret offered a great explanation about how to use this fly:

"This pattern is customarily used to pursue landlocked salmon during ice-out and the spring months when the water is still cool and fish are near the top of the water column. As with many of Carrie Stevens's patterns, this fly imitates a smelt, a favorite food of the salmon. Tied in this manner, it is customarily trolled. Other variations for casting are tied on hooks made with shorter shanks."

Supervisor

tied by Garret Booth
Temple, New Hampshire

According to Garret Booth, "I am neither a guide nor have a fly shop. I'm a commercial tier, and have been in business now for three years. I hope to incorporate guiding into the business, as soon as I find time to get away from the vise long enough in the summer."

Regardless of whether he is a guide, Garret is a supremely accomplished tier.

"I offer tying and casting classes, either individually or as a group. I also offer over five hundred patterns of flies. Many orders are tied according to customer specifications since they will be *their* tools with which to work."

Garret Booth's rendition of the Supervisor, another of Carrie Stevens's famous patterns, shows his obvious flare for tying streamers. The Supervisor is a good choice for catching landlocked salmon and trout, especially in the spring when the trophy fish are feeding on smelt. Garret recommends tying the fly on long-shank hooks for trolling; use shorter-shank hooks if you plan to cast these flies.

Hook: Partridge Carrie Stevens streamer hook, size 4.
Thread: Black 8/0, with a band of red thread in the middle of the head.
Tail: Red hackle fibers.
Body: Flat silver tinsel.
Rib: Oval silver tinsel.
Throat: White bucktail, then light blue and white hackle fibers.
Underwing: Four to six strands of peacock herl.
Wings: Four light blue saddle hackles, two hackles per wing.
Shoulders: Pale green saddle hackles, one-third the length of the wings.
Cheeks: Jungle cock.

Yellow-tail Olive Crystal Bugger

tied by Peter J. Bauer
Gardnerville, Nevada

Hook: Tiemco TMC5263, sizes 8 to 2.
Thread: Black 6/0.
Head: Gold bead.
Tail: Yellow marabou and a couple of strands of pearl Krystal Flash.
Body: Olive New Age Chenille (Crystal Chenille is a good substitute).
Hackle: Grizzly dyed chartreuse.

This is my most popular and productive Woolly Bugger," says Guide Peter Bauer. "Fish it with a stripping retrieve. It's a good searching pattern for lakes."

The Woolly Bugger remains one of the all-time best producers of trout, salmon, bass—almost all species of freshwater fish—that has ever been devised. It's also one of the most common patterns tied in beginning fly-tying classes. If you're new to tying, whip up a couple copies of Peter Bauer's Yellow-tail Olive Crystal Bugger.

Midnight Mac

tied by Mac McGee
Chattanooga, Tennessee

Hook: Salmon or steelhead hook, size 6.
Thread: Black 3/0.
Tail: Black Zonker strip with stands of blue holographic Flashabou.
Body: Black, blue, or red Crystal Chenille, with a black hackle palmered up the shank.
Hackle: Grizzly.
Eyes: Small dumbbell eyes.

Mac uses this pattern in the fall and winter to catch trout, and in the fall to catch steelhead. It's a variation of the ever-popular Woolly Bugger, but the rabbit-strip tail makes it a bit tougher.

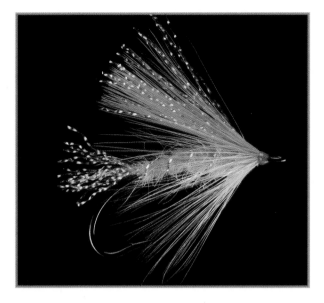
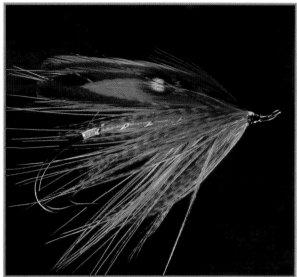

Home Run

tied by Rich Youngers
Salem, Oregon

Hook: Daiichi 2151, sizes 2 and 1 for steelhead; Tiemco TMC7999, sizes 10 and 8 for sea-run cutthroat trout.
Thread: Fire-orange 8/0.
Tail: Flat silver tinsel.
Tail: Pink Krystal Flash.
Body: Rear two-thirds, hot pink SLF dubbing; front one-third, hot orange SLF dubbing.
Underwing: Hot orange marabou.
Wing: Hot orange Krystal Flash
Collar: Hot pink hen hackle.

When I started this project recording favorite guide flies, my plan was to not include steelhead patterns. The reason was simple: I don't know anything about fishing for steelhead, and a writer should stick to what he knows. But then Rich Youngers sent three lovely steelhead flies, and I knew I just had to include them in this collection. So while I still can't say much about fishing for steelhead, I can say something about Rich's flies: they're first rate.

"This pattern is a great winter-run steelhead fly for off-color water conditions," says Rich Youngers. "This fly is tied sparse with body blends of SLF dubbing that pick up light well even in dingy water. The hook is made of heavy wire so the fly sinks quickly."

The Home Run attests to the prevalence of some steelhead anglers to choose bright patterns. The Krystal Flash in the wing and tail really makes this fly stand out. The collar is swept back—a sign that the tier really knows his business—and the head is remarkably small. Flies like this make me want to learn more about steelhead fishing.

D.C. Cutthroat Spey

tied by Rich Youngers
Salem, Oregon

Hook: Daiichi 2051, sizes 7 to 1.5.
Thread: Black or hot orange 8/0.
Tag: Flat silver tinsel.
Body: Rear two-thirds, hot orange silk floss; front one-third, hot orange dubbing.
Hackle: Blue-eared pheasant dyed hot orange.
Collar: Gadwall or widgeon dyed hot orange.
Wing: Black-laced hen hackle dyed orange.
Cheeks: Tragopan or jungle cock.

Dr. Tom Whiting, of Whiting Farms, is the world's leading producer of fine hackle. Tom is always pushing the envelope and developing new feathers for us to use. A few years ago, he introduced his line of laced hackles. These feathers have fine black lines on the edges, and can be used to create some outstanding effects on your flies. A good example is the wing on Rich Youngers's D.C. Cutthroat Spey; the black edge silhouettes the wing.

Rich says this about the D.C. Cutthroat Spey:

"This pattern was originally developed for fishing small coastal Oregon Streams that have runs of sea-run cutthroat trout. It is tied in small sizes to imitate the crayfish that live in these streams. I have also used it in larger sizes to trick wild steelhead. The fly was named for one of my favorite small coastal steelhead and cutthroat streams."

Santiam Spey

tied by Rich Youngers
Salem, Oregon

Hook: Daiichi 2051, sizes 3 to 1.5.
Thread: Black 8/0.
Tag: Flat silver tinsel.
Body: Rear one-third, hot pink floss, over which is tied a pair of jungle-cock feathers back to back; middle one-third, lavender dubbing; front one-third, purple dubbing.
Hackle: Blue-eared pheasant dyed purple.
Collar: Widgeon or gadwall dyed purple.
Wing: Bronze mallard flack dyed purple.

This fly was developed for fishing the gin-clear waters of the North Santium River located east of Salem, Oregon," says Rich Youngers. "North Santium steelhead prefer larger flies, and purple is the go-to color on all of Oregon's Willamette Valley streams."

Youngers fishes the Santium Spey with a 7- or 8-weight rod, and a stout, 10- to 12-pound-test leader.

In addition to fishing the North Santium, Rich and the guys at Creekside Fly Fishing guide on the Deschutes and McKenzie Rivers.

Montreal Whore

tied by Dan Legere
Greenville, Maine

Hook: Long-shank streamer hook, sizes 10 to 2.
Thread: Black 6/0.
Body: Orange wool.
Rib: Flat silver tinsel.
Underwing: Red, white, and blue bucktail.
Wing: White marabou.

Dan Legere, who has owned his fly shop in Greenville, Maine, for nearly twenty years, is one of the Pinetree State's leading guides. He specializes on fishing the West Branch of the Penobscot and East Outlet of the Kennebec Rivers. His forte is catching the region's trophy landlocked salmon, and he can also put you into some nice brook trout. In addition to these two major rivers, the Moosehead Lake area includes the Roach River, the Moose River, and dozens of excellent trout ponds. You could spend a couple of weeks in Greenville and fish a new piece of water every day.

The Montreal Whore was developed by Lenny Loiselle, and is a general attractor streamer; at most, it's a loose imitation of a smelt. Tie the marabou wing rather full to give the fly a lot of swimming movement in the water. Dan prefers fishing the Montreal Whore down-and-across stream, and retrieves the fly with short strips.

Kuss Bug

tied by Mary Kuss
Media, Pennsylvania

Hook: Regular wet-fly hook, size 10.
Thread: Orange 3/0.
Tail: Tan marabou.
Body: Tan chenille.
Legs: Brown round rubber legs.
Back: Brown chenille.

Mary Kuss, an experienced guide working out of The Sporting Gentleman, a great shop in Media, Pennsylvania, ties this lightweight panfish pattern. This fly catches bass, but also works on perch and other warmwater species.

Fish the Kuss Bug with a 5- or 6-weight rod, and 4X or 5X leader. Mary says this pattern is an excellent generic imitation nymph imitation.

Fur Ball

tied by Capt. Pat Ehlers
Milwaukee, Wisconsin

Hook: Regular stainless-steel hook, size 4.
Thread: Size 6/0, color to match the body material.
Tail: SAAP wing material and a grizzly hackle on each side of the tail.
Body: SAAP body fur.
Eyes: Medium dome eyes coated with epoxy.

Pat Ehlers, representing a shop called The Fly Fishers, uses the Fur Ball to catch smallmouth bass on the Great Lakes and local rivers, and for pike, muskie, and bass in the other local lakes. He has also used the Fur Ball to catch salmon, steelhead, tarpon, snook, and jacks. Pat says that the Fur Ball "is a general baitfish imitation that pushes a lot of water."

The synthetic hair used to tie the Fur Ball makes this a very durable pattern. Tie the Fur Ball in a variety of your favorite fish-catching colors.

Pat uses a 6- to 9-weight outfit to fish the Fur Ball. When he needs to go deep, he switches to a sinking-tip or full-sinking line.

Hook: Regular stainless-steel hook, size 4.
Thread: Red 6/0.
Wing & tail: Red or chartreuse Zonker strip.
Body: White crosscut rabbit strip.
Sides: Krystal Flash and rubber legs.
Eyes: Medium silver dome eyes coated with epoxy.

Maverick Minnow

tied by Capt. Pat Ehlers
Milwaukee, Wisconsin

This is one of Pat Ehlers' favorite flies for catching bass, pike, salmon, steelhead, tarpon, snook, and redfish.

Tie the Zonker strip on the hook shank opposite the hook barb. Tie on the body rabbit strip and wrap up the shank. Pull the forward portion of the Zonker strip over the top of the body, tie down, and clip the excess.

Pat uses the Maverick Minnow anytime of the day throughout the season. He strips the fly through the water to mimic a swimming baitfish.

Murray's Blue Damsel Dry Skater

tied by Harry Murray
Edinburg, Virginia

Harry Murray is an expert at fishing for Virginia's smallmouth bass and panfish. His Blue Damsel Dry Skater is the perfect pattern to use when real damselflies are flittering around the water.

This fly is not complicated to tie. Use general dry-fly tying methods with bright blue materials. Fish this fly with a skating motion across the surface of the water. It can also be fished dead-drift.

Hook: Long-shank dry-fly hook, sizes 8 and 6.
Thread: Blue 6/0.
Tail: Blue calftail.
Body: Blue dubbing.
Hackle: Blue dry-fly hackle.

Murray's Strymph

tied by Harry Murray
Edinburg, Virginia

Hook: 3X-long wet-fly hook, sizes 10 to 4.
Thread: Olive 3/0.
Weight: Lead wire.
Tail: Olive ostrich herl.
Body: Olive rabbit fur dubbing.
Hackle: Olive hen hackle.

Murray's Strymph is an imitation of a leech. Tie it small and use lightweight tackle to catch trout, or dress it larger and use heavy tackle to drag bass out of the weeds.

Murray's Strymph is a good fly for novice tiers. You may substitute olive chenille for the body if you haven't gotten the hang of wrapping a dubbed body.

Fish Murray's Strymph with a slow, stripping retrieve to imitate a swimming leech.

Murray's Lead-Eye Hellgrammite

tied by Harry Murray
Edinburg, Virginia

Hook: 3X-long wet-fly hook, sizes 8 to 4.
Thread: Black 3/0.
Weight: Medium lead dumbbell eyes.
Tail: Black ostrich herl.
Body: Black chenille.
Hackle: Black saddle hackle.
Pinchers: Rubber hackle.

Murray's Hellgrammite first appeared in *Fly Tyer* magazine many years ago. It's a variation of a Woolly Bugger, and it is an excellent bass fly. When tied in smaller sizes, it's perfect for catching panfish and even trout.

Because of the heavy lead eyes, you'll want to fish Murray's Hellgrammite using a stout rod. Select a 6-weight rod to cast small versions of the fly; a 7- or 8-weight rod is best for larger flies. Fish this pattern with a jerking retrieve, and allow it to sink between strips of line.

Murray's Mad Tom Sculpin

tied by Harry Murray
Edinburg, Virginia

Hook: 4X-long streamer hook, sizes 8 to 4.
Thread: Black 3/0.
Eyes: Small lead dumbbell eyes.
Tail: Black rabbit strip.
Body: Black rabbit dubbing.
Fins: Black, shaggy dubbing.
Head: Black rabbit dubbing.

Harry Murray uses this fly throughout the year. He says that it's an "excellent pattern for large trout in deep pools in large rivers, and for large smallmouths in deep pools and deep cuts."

Murray fishes these flies with a 6- to 9-weight rod, a floating or sinking-tip line, and 9-foot-long leaders with a 3X tippet.

When tying Murray's Mad Tom Sculpin, add a considerable amount of rabbit dubbing to the thread (a dubbing loop is the easiest method). Attempt to tie a tapered body that gets narrower near the rabbit-strip tail. The soft, flowing tail gives the fly a lot of lifelike action in the water.

Ghost Minn-O

tied by Thomas Baltz
Mt. Holly Springs, Pennsylvania

Hook: Mustad 3366, size 4.
Thread: Yellow 3/0 Monocord.
Tail: White Ultra hair, four strands of root beer Krystal Flash, and tan Ultra Hair.
Body: Pearl-olive Estaz.
Wing: Tan Ultra Hair.
Throat: Four to five strands of red Krystal Flash.
Head: Yellow deer hair, spun and clipped to shape.
Eyes: Extra-small doll eyes glued to the sides of the head.

"I created this fly to use for smallmouth bass during the low, clear water periods of summer and fall on the Susquehanna and Juniata rivers," says Tom Baltz. "The fly offers a subtle, translucent look with sort of a neutral buoyancy, much like a natural minnow. This color scheme does not imitate any specific baitfish, but it seems to appeal to the bass. I have also tied this fly in white, chartreuse, and orange color schemes, but this one is my favorite."

Guide Tom Baltz also has some specific recommendations about how to fish this fly.

"I like to fish this fly with a nine-foot rod, a seven-weight line, and a long leader—twelve feet or more. Fluorocarbon tippet material is a good idea. Always tie the fly to the tippet with an open-loop knot. Dead-drifting the fly with occasional six-inch pulls—not jerks—has been the most effective at enticing strikes."

Hook: 4X-long streamer hook, sizes 8 and 6.
Thread: Black 3/0 Monocord.
Tail: Black marabou and strands of Flashabou.
Body: Pearl-black Crystal Chenille.
Hackle: Black, spiral-wrapped over the body.
Collar & head: Black deer hair, spun and clipped to shape.

Mudd-Bugger

tied by Thomas Baltz
Mt. Holly Springs, Pennsylvania

This fly is black, but guide Tom Baltz recommends tying it in a variety of colors, and olive would be especially effective.

"This pattern evolved from an idea to spin a deer-hair collar on the head of a Woolly Bugger to increase the amount of water the fly would push," says Baltz. "I originally tied it for smallmouth bass, but it has been quite effective for trout as well. For trout, I clamp a split-shot at the head of the fly and fish it deep. It has a sculpin look to it. I also fish it at the surface for bass—waking style—and sometimes incorporate a section of lead-core line into the leader and run a tippet off of that so the lead core scrapes the bottom, but the fly rides somewhat above it."

Creeping Crawdad

tied by Justin Moeykens
New Boston, New Hampshire

Lots of streams and almost all lakes have good populations of crayfish, and they are a favorite food of large fish. Some crayfish imitations are complicated to tie, but Justin Moeykens's Creeping Crawdad is easy. When tying this fly, he says "the eyes need to be tied on top of the shank so the hook rides point up. And the rabbit strip claw is not tied in, rather the hook point is punched through the hide. This allows for more motion and the ability to quickly change the color of the strip."

Fish the Creeping Crawdad any time of the day throughout the season. Justin says that "the fly fishes best bumped along the bottom with a short stripping retrieve."

Hook: Tiemco TMC3761, sizes 8 to 4.
Thread: Camel 8/0.
Eyes: Plated lead eyes.
Antennae: A mix of bronze Flashabou and root beer Krystal Flash.
Body: Brown rabbit dubbing.
Legs: A long, soft grouse feather.
Claw: A natural rabbit strip.

Hook: Long-shank saltwater hook, sizes
4/0 to 2/0.
Thread: Black 3/0.
Tail: Gold holographic saltwater
Flashabou.
Body: Yellow crosscut rabbit strip.
Eyes: Yellow and red paint.

Yellow Muskie Bunny

tied by Dan Legere
Greenville, Maine

Dan Legere, the owner of Maine Guide Fly Shop, occasionally fishes for muskie at Maine's Baker Lake. I've traveled to Baker Lake, which is near the border with Quebec, and the muskies are very large. These fish demand big flies, and the Yellow Muskie Bunny is a good choice. In addition to the yellow version, Dan also ties this fly in chartreuse and white. Fish these large patterns in the spring and fall with a floating line and a stripping retrieve.

Chartreuse Slimsnake

tied by Todd Polacek
Madison, Wisconsin

The Slimsnake is used to catch smallmouth bass and muskies. Be sure to use a wire tippet when fishing for muskie.

"Bang this fly against the banks and behind rocks," says Todd Polacek. "Give it two strips. If you don't catch anything, cast it to the next place. Don't bring it all the way to the boat."

Polacek uses a 7- or 8-weight rod and a floating rod. When it comes to fishing for muskie, he uses a 10-pound-test leader and a length of steel wire. This combination lets him cast this big fly and fight these fierce fish.

Hook: Regular saltwater hook, size 1/0.
Thread: Chartreuse 6/0.
Eyes: Chrome dumbbell eyes.
Tail: A chartreuse marabou feather.
Body: A chartreuse Zonker strip.

~SALTWATER~
GUIDE FLIES

Cowen's "Natural" Baitfish

tied by Henry Cowen
Gainesville, Georgia

Hook: Regular saltwater hook, sizes 2 to 2/0.
Thread: Fine clear monofilament.
Weight: Medium lead wire.
Body: Pearl braid.
Tail: White Polafibre.
Wing: Lavender Slinky Flash and olive Slinky Flash.
Belly: White Slinky Flash.
Throat: Hot pink Flurofibre.
Eyes: Large silver dome eyes epoxied to the sides of the head.

I first met Henry Cowen at the International Fly Tying Symposium in Somerset, New Jersey. The International Fly Tying Symposium is an annual event dedicated to the art of fly tying. Tiers come from all over the world to participate in this great show; it's one of the best places to learn all of the finer points of tying beautiful, fishing-catching flies. Henry usually ties saltwater patterns at the symposium, and he supplies all of us with bagels every morning.

Cowen's "Natural" Baitfish is an excellent example of Henry's durable and inventive patterns. He uses this fly to catch a wide variety of fish: striped bass, weakfish, bluefish, false albacore, snook, tarpon, and freshwater bass. Henry says that this fly imitates many wide-bodied baitfish, and it's his "number one pattern when the fish are below ten feet deep. Fish this fly with a slow but steady retrieve, and give it time to sink."

Cowen's Phat Lip

tied by Henry Cowen
Gainesville, Georgia

Hook: Long-shank saltwater hook, size 2/0.
Thread: Fine clear monofilament.
Tail: White saddle hackles and pearl Krystal Flash.
Throat: Red Crystal Chenille.
Head: Edgewater 1/0 small Boilermaker foam head covered with ½-inch-diameter clear Fly Flex tubing and coated with epoxy.
Eyes: Medium silver holographic adhesive eyes.

Here's a lightweight pattern that has a lot of action in the water. The stiff lip causes the fly to dart and wiggle, and it pushes a lot of water.

"For brackish, stained water, I tie this fly in yellow, and it is deadly," says Henry Cowen. Both the color and the movement allow gamefish to pick up on its trail.

Making the head and lip of this fly is easier than you might think. Slip the foam head onto the hook, and tie on the tail and collar. Next, slip a piece of Flex Fly tubing onto the foam. Tie off the tubing behind the hook eye, and pull the excess tubing down to form the lip. Add the eyes and coat the head with epoxy.

Cowen fishes the Phat lip with a 9-weight rod and an intermediate-sinking line. A pattern with this type of lip can be tough to pick up off the water and cast; the lip causes the fly to dig down. That's one reason you'll want to use a stout rod when fishing this fly; another is that it can catch really big fish.

Cowen's Magnum Baitfish

tied by Henry Cowen
Gainesville, Georgia

Hook: Short-shank saltwater hook, size 4/0.
Thread: Fine clear monofilament.
Body: Olive, lavender, and white Slinky/Flash
Throat: Pink Fluro Fibre.
Eyes: Extra-large dome holographic eyes.

I can't resist saying it: big fish eat big little fish. And Cowen's Magnum Baitfish is a big fly.

The Magnum Baitfish is perfect for catching stripped bass, bluefish, and any other fish that feeds on bunker. Tie the Magnum Baitfish primarily in olive to imitate shad; tie it in blue, and it is a good forgery of a herring. On April 4, 2002, a version of this pattern was used to catch the 20-pound-class-tippet world record striped bass at Rarity Bay, New Jersey. That fish weighed 36.4 pounds.

Henry Cowen says he prefers fishing this pattern with an intermediate-sinking or fast-sinking line.

Cowen's Transformer

tied by Henry Cowen
Gainesville, Georgia

Hook: Long-shank saltwater hook, size 2/0.
Thread: Fine clear monofilament.
Tail: White bucktail.
Wing: Olive bucktail and strands of pearl Flashabou or a similar material.
Eyes: Medium dumbbell eyes tied on top of the hook shank.
Popping Head: Live Body Foam or a similar closed-cell foam. Make a slit to the middle of the foam, place the foam onto the leader, and slide the popping head down to the head of the fly.

"I was with a friend on the beach in Westport, Connecticut, back in June, 1993, when we saw fish moving into the wash," says Henry Cowen. "We were fishing poppers. When the fish raced by us, we had about six to eight casts each without any takes. By the time I tried to re-rig, the fish had long since moved off the beach. That night I knew I wanted a fly that could let me go from fishing the surface to fishing subsurface without the time involved in changing flies, and I created the Transformer. Now if I am in the same situation, with only a few shots at fast-moving fish, I can quickly change from a popper to a Clouser-style fly without tying any knots! Just slide the popping head onto the leader and slip it down onto the head of the fly. It works like a charm!"

Hook: Regular saltwater hook, size 2 to 2/0.
Thread: Fine monofilament thread.
Tail: White Zonker strip and pearl Krystal Flash.
Body: Gold braid.
Wing: Pink and olive bucktail.
Eye: Small dumbbell eyes.
Spinner: Size OO Colorado spinner blade attached to a size O barrel swivel.

Cowen's Coyote

tied by Henry Cowen
Gainesville, Georgia

Using spinner blades on flies is a very old technique, and it works very well. The blades give flies a little additional flash and sound in the water. As Henry Cowen explains, "This fly was designed to imitate a Blakemore Roadrunner. For those not familiar with the Roadrunner, it is nothing more than a bucktail jig with a spinner in front to give vibration and flash. A Blakemore Roadrunner is, in my opinion, the most consistent fish-catching lure for conventional-tackle fishermen. Now we have one for fly fishermen."

Joe Scandore, a friend of Henry's, tells another story about the success of the Coyote.

"I was standing on a sandbar on at the mouth of the Housatonic River in April. There were six other fishermen around me, but I was the only one standing in the middle. As the tide started moving out, I began catching stripers in the three- to five-pound range. By the time the tide began to slow down, the total number of fish caught was approximately twenty by all anglers. I caught at least fourteen myself, and the other six fishermen totaled six fish. No one else caught a fish until I handed Coyotes to two of the other anglers."

With the eyes tied on top of the hook shank, the Coyote flips over in the water and fishes like a Clouser Minnow. Henry Cowen says that the Coyote, which is sold by Umpqua Feather Merchants, catches just about anything that swims, including striped bass, cobia, bonefish, baby tarpon, snook, false albacore, and freshwater bass.

Flower Land

tied by Deborah Duran
Taunton, Massachusetts

I've been meeting the nice folks from the Bear's Den Fly Shop, of Taunton, Massachusetts, off and on for the past several years. The Bear's Den sent several patterns, all tied by Deborah Duran. These are some of the most beautiful saltwater flies I've ever seen, and I'm very happy to include them in this collection of guide flies.

The Flower Land is not only a very attractive fly, but is a great streamer for catching a wide variety of fish.

Hook: Orvis 751Q, size 2/0.
Thread: Black Flat-Waxed Nylon.
Body: Silver Bill's Bodi Braid.
Wing: Soft-yellow bucktail topped with orange and purple bucktail, and peacock herl on top. Add strands of very fine copper and pearl Flashabou type material.
Throat: White marabou.
Eyes: Extra-small silver adhesive eyes. Give the head a generous coating of cement to protect the eyes.

Indian Puddle

tied by Deborah Duran
Taunton, Massachusetts

Hook: Orvis 751Q, size 2/0.
Thread: Black Flat-Waxed Nylon.
Body: Fluorescent orange Sparkle Braid.
Wing: Fluorescent orange bucktail topped with golden yellow bucktail, claret bucktail, and rootbeer Krystal Flash.
Throat: Fluorescent fire-orange marabou.
Cheeks: Gold Angel Hair.
Eyes: Extra-small silver adhesive eyes.

The Indian Puddle is an obvious cousin to the beautiful Flower Land. This is another attractive streamer that fishes as good as it looks.

Butterfly Fish

tied by Deborah Duran
Taunton, Massachusetts

Hook: Red Big Fly thread.
Body: Pearl Mirage Krystal Flash tied splayed and flanked on each side by a pheasant feather.
Topping: Peacock sword fibers.
Throat: Red Krystal Flash.
Eyes: Small white dome eyes.

This is one of the most beautiful and unusual patterns in the book. I don't know if you'll want to tie and fish this fly, but it sure is nice to look at.

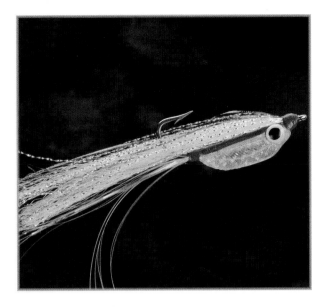

Chartreuse Rattler

tied by Deborah Duran
Taunton, Massachusetts

Hook: Mustad 34011, size 1.
Thread: Red Big Fly thread.
Eyes: Medium lead dumbbell eyes painted yellow with black pupils.
Tail: Pearl Flashabou.
Body: Chartreuse E-Z Body Tubing with a glass rattle.
Wing: Chartreuse Super Hair, chartreuse Krystal Flash, and green Fire Fly.

This is another of Deborah Duran's attractive and fun-to-tie patterns. The Chartreuse Rattler is not as difficult to make as you might think.

Begin by tying on the eyes and tail. Next, tie on a piece of E-Z Body Tubing at the base of the tail. Insert a glass rattle into the tubing, tie the front of the tubing off in front of the eyes, and clip the excess. Coat the tubing and eyes with epoxy. Allow the epoxy to dry, and tie on the wing.

The Chartreuse Rattler is a tad heavy, so you'll want to use a stout rod—maybe a 9-weight—to cast this pattern.

The Final Thing

tied by Capt. Tom McQuade
St. John, Virgin Islands

Hook: Regular saltwater hook, size 6.
Thread: Fine clear monofilament.
Feelers: Grizzly Sili Legs and two grizzly hackles.
Eyes: Two small copper beads glued to pieces of monofilament.
Weight: Small lead dumbbell eyes.
Body: Grizzly hackle spiral-wrapped on the hook shank and clipped to shape.
Back: Peacock feather.
Weed guard: 25-pound-test monofilament.

Tom McQuade, a guide living in the Virgin Islands, ties a variety of inventive crustacean patterns. I featured several of his flies in my previous book, *Tying Contemporary Saltwater Flies*.

Tom ties flies that imitate the multitude of crustaceans inhabiting the waters of the Virgin Islands. He says he doesn't know the names of some of these critters, so refers to them as "things." His patterns include The Thing, The Other Thing, and now The Final Thing. While Tom's not sure what the real crustaceans are called, he does know that they are an important source of food for the local bonefish.

For a more complete description of Capt. McQuad's flies, check out the article I wrote for the Spring 2003 issue of *Fly Tyer* magazine. That article is titled "Virgin Islands Beauties," and it contains an interview in which Tom describes fishing in his part of paradise and his theories about fly tying.

Hook: Regular saltwater hook, size 1.
Thread: White 3/0.
Body: White, pink, and olive marabou, craft fur, or Angel Hair with strands of ultra violet Krystal Flash.
Head: Softex.
Gills: Red permanent marker.
Eyes: Small silver adhesive eyes.

Swimmy

tied by Ben Furimsky
Crested Butte, Colorado

The Swimmy is a good imitation of a spearing or bay anchovy. It's an especially good fly to use when fishing for striped bass and false albacore. Although Ben Furimsky lives in Colorado, he often visits the Northeast and fishes the Atlantic Coast.

Begin the Swimmy by tying on all of the soft body materials facing forward over the hook eye. Tie off and clip the thread. Next, fold back the materials and place an eye on each side of the head, and coat the head with Softex. Allow the Softex to dry, and add the gills.

The Swimmy is a lightweight pattern that should be fished with a slow, stripping retrieve.

Shine Tail

tied by Ben Furimsky
Crested Butte, Colorado

Bugskin is a very durable leather fly-tying material. It comes in many colors and can be used to make many parts on flies.

To tie the Shine Tail, cut the Bugskin into the shape of a small baitfish. Slip the Bugskin into the tubing, and slip the tubing onto the hook shank. Tie off the nose of the Shine Tail behind the hook eye, and tie down the end of the body at the base of the tail. Add the silver adhesive eyes and gills, and coat the head with epoxy.

Use Bugskin and Corsair Tubing to create a variety of baitfish imitations.

Hook: Regular saltwater hook, size 1/0.
Thread: White 3/0.
Body: Flash Bugskin and Corsair Tubing.
Gills: Red permanent marker.
Eyes: Small silver adhesive eyes.

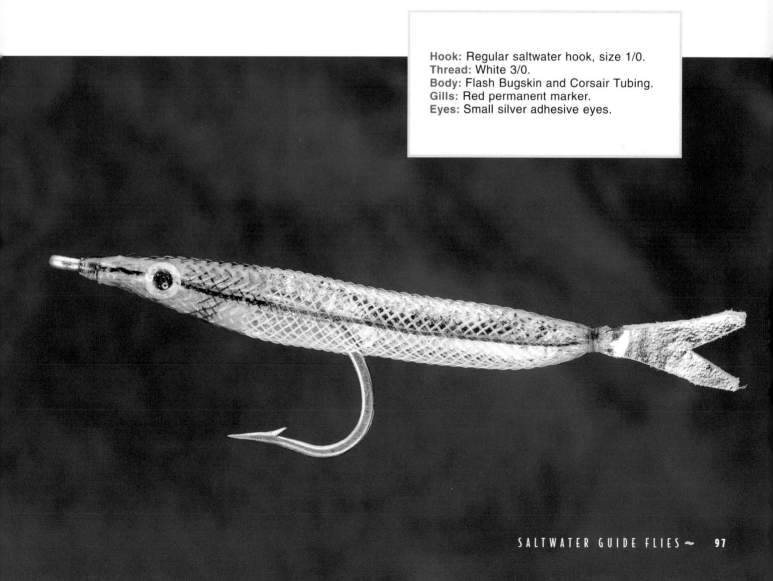

Hook: Regular saltwater hook, size 2 or 1.
Thread: Olive 3/0.
Tail: Gold Flashabou.
Body: Rootbeer Estaz and ginger hackle spiral wrapped up the hook shank.
Eyes: Medium dumbbell eyes.
Weed guard: 45-pound-test monofilament.

Savannah Fly

tied by Capt. Scott Wagner
Thunderbolt, Georgia

Capt. Wagner's guide service is called Savannah Fly. He has the run of about a hundred miles of undeveloped coastline featuring grass and mud flats. Capt. Wagner reports that there is little competition for the redfish on the flats where he fishes, and that "the few flats boats in this area don't even have pushpoles."

The Savannah Fly is a good choice when fishing for redfish, sea trout, and ladyfish. It's a bright fly and easy to tie, perfect for novice tiers eager to create some basic flies that catch fish.

Capt. Wagner uses the Savannah Fly throughout the year. He recommends using either a slow or fast retrieve, and a 7- through 9-weight rod. He also varies the length of the leader—from six to nine feet long—depending upon the clarity of the water.

Striper Head Fake

tied by Capt. Scott Wagner
Thunderbolt, Georgia

Hook: Regular saltwater hook, size 3/0.
Thread: Olive 3/0.
Tail: Silver Krystal Flash, white bucktail, grizzly hackle, and peacock herl.
Body: White wool yarn, and grizzly hackle spiral wrapped over the body.
Eyes: Medium dumbbell eyes.

The Georgia Coast hosts runs of very large striped bass, and Capt. Wagner is in the middle of the action. The Striper Head Fake, which he tied to imitate a small shad, is one of the patterns he uses to catch these fish.

"And if you really want to test your tackle," says Capt. Wagner, "we have a huge push of large jack cravelle in the summer. I don't tie anything fancy for them due to their nature for wrecking everything thrown at them. These jacks average around twenty pounds, with many caught in the upper twenties and low thirties."

Bonefish Slider

tied by Capt. Kent Gibbens
Ormond Beach, Florida

Hook: Tiemco TMC811S, sizes 2 and 1.
Thread: White Flat-Waxed Nylon.
Tail: Tan Fly Fur and strands of pearl Krystal Flash on top. Use a brown permanent marker to add stripes to the tail.
Head & collar: Deer hair, spun and clipped to shape.
Eyes: Small lead dumbbell eyes. Use enamel paint to add eyes to the dumbbells.
Weed guard: 15-pound-test monofilament.

Capt. Gibbens uses Tim Borski's Bonefish Slider to catch sea trout, redfish, snook and baby tarpon in the Mosquito Lagoon and Indian River areas. He uses a 7- to 9-weight rod, and either a floating or intermediate-sinking line. He is also partial to very long leaders; if the water is very clear, he'll use a leader as long as thirteen feet.

Tim Borski tells the story of the Bonefish Slider in the Winter 2000 issue of the *Redbone Journal*. Tim says that the Bonefish Slider owes its origins to Don Gapen's Muddler Minnow. This explains the clipped deer-hair head on the Bonefish Slider. He says this fly is a saltwater version of Gapen's very famous pattern.

Mr. Tasty Toad

tied by Capt. Kent Gibbens
Ormond Beach, Florida

Hook: Mustad 34007, sizes 4 to 2/0.
Thread: Chartreuse 6/0.
Tail: White marabou on the bottom, tan marabou in the middle, and olive marabou on the top.
Body: White and olive polypropylene yarn.
Eyes: Medium lead dumbbell eyes.

Capt. Harry Spear originated this fly. It's a very effective bonefish pattern, and it will also do a number on the sea trout and redfish. It's very simple to tie, and even a novice will quickly get the hang of this pattern and create fish-catching Toads.

Experiment by the tying the pattern in a variety of colors: olive, light olive, and tan. You can also create flies with different sink rates by using various sizes of dumbbell eyes.

Capt. Gibbens recommends fishing Mr. Tasty Toad on the bottom with a very slow strip retrieve.

Gibbens "Go-To" Fly

tied by Capt. Kent Gibbens
Ormond Beach, Florida

Hook: Regular saltwater hook, sizes 2 to 1/0.
Thread: White 3/0.
Tail: Grizzly saddle hackles, tied splayed.
Collar & head: White and red deer hair, spun and clipped to shape.
Eyes: Small eyes painted on the sides of the head.

This pattern, tied by Keith Beach, is Capt. Gibbens "go-to" floating fly. Here we see it tied in the classic colors red and white, but yellow and green, and red and yellow, are also very effective. Capt. Gibbens fishes this fly with a floating line and a hard type leader with a 20-pound-test bite tippet. He reports that this is an excellent snook and tarpon pattern when fishing the backcountry.

Obsession Eel

tied by Capt. Dave Pecci
Bath, Maine

Capt. Dave Pecci is one of Maine's most experienced saltwater guides. I've fished with Dave twice. The first time we motored about twenty miles offshore to catch blue sharks. We caught several that day, including one that pushed 100 pounds. Another time we fished the lower Kennebec River for striped bass. The Kennebec has been getting big runs of stripers, and Capt. Pecci knows all of the ins and outs of the river.

The problem with fishing the lower Kennebec, however, is that it sometimes gets monstrous runs of bait. This can be frustrating because in their mad dash to gobble a meal, the bass can miss your fly. The time I fished with Dave, we could see huge spiraling tornadoes of herring in the water. The bass were pushing the herring against the rocks and ripping into the bait; there were explosions of water where the stripers were attacking the herring. We tried a variety of patterns, and also used fast-sinking lines to get our flies below the schools of bait. We did catch a couple of bass, but with all of the herring in the water, our offerings went largely ignored.

Dave's Obsession Eel is simple to tie and very effective for catching striped bass and bluefish. Dave adds a few wraps of lead wire to the hook shank before tying the fly. He then ties on an 8-inch-long Zonker strip, wraps the strip twice around the hook to create the collar, and then ties off and clips the excess strip. Next, he ties on a large piece of E-Z Body tubing, and ties off and clips the thread. Dave then pushes the tubing back on itself, and starts the thread on top of the tubing. Pull the thread tight to compress the head behind the hook shank, and clip the excess tubing. Now tie off and clip the thread, and epoxy the eyes in place.

The rabbit-strip tail and collar give this pattern a lot of action in the water. The rabbit strip and E-Z Body tubing are also very durable. If you tie this fly well, you will be able to fish it all day without it coming apart.

> **Hook:** Regular saltwater hook, size 4/0.
> **Thread:** Black 3/0.
> **Body:** Black or olive Zonker strip.
> **Head:** Black or black/pearl E-Z Body tubing.
> **Eyes:** Extra-small doll eyes epoxied to the sides of the head.

Obsession Green Crab

tied by Capt. Dave Pecci
Bath, Maine

Hook: Regular saltwater hook, size 2.
Thread: Black 3/0.
Weight: Large dumbbell eyes tied to the top of the hook shank.
Body: Olive Zonker strip wrapped up the hook shank.
Eyes: Melted monofilament.
Claws: Grizzly hackle dyed green, clipped to shape and coated with head cement.

I'll bet crab patterns are some of the most overlooked flies in the upper Northeast, but striped bass do indeed feed on crabs. Capt. Pecci's Obsession Green Crab is a good candidate for your fly box if you'd like to try this style of fly. He fishes it throughout the midsummer and throughout the day—even under bright light conditions—and uses short strips of line to keep the fly near the bottom.

This fly is very simple to tie. Just lash on the dumbbell eyes, monofilament eyes, and the claws. Next, tie a Zonker strip to the end of the shank. Advance the thread to behind the hook eye. Wrap the rabbit strip up the hook, tie off, and clip.

While Capt. Pecci uses this pattern in the Northeast, it will also make an excellent fly for casting to bonefish and permit. Change the color of the Zonker strip to match the popular crab patterns in the area where you fish. A barred rabbit strip would give the finished fly a natural mottled appearance.

Mangrove Muddler

tied by Capt. Al Keller
Naples, Florida

Hook: Long-shank saltwater hook, sizes 2 to 1/0.
Thread: Brown 3/0.
Tail: Copper Wing N' Flash.
Body: Gold braid.
Wing: Yellow marabou, pearl Krystal Flash, and two grizzly hackles.
Topping: Peacock herl.
Head: Natural deer hair, spun and clipped to shape.

Yes, Marabou Muddlers work in the salt. Capt. Al Keller uses his Mangrove Muddler to catch tarpon, snook, and redfish throughout the year. In addition to the colors seen here, Capt. Keller also ties this pattern in black and tan, white and red, and all gray. He says this pattern does a fine job of imitating mullet and other small baitfish, and he fishes it with a stripping retrieve.

Capt. Keller guides out of the Everglades Angler, a shop located at the Hyatt Regency Coconut Point Resort & Spa in Bonita Springs, Florida. The guides at the shop specialize in fishing the 10,000 Islands and Everglades National Park.

Capt. Ray's Angel Hair Silverside

tied by Capt. Ray Stachelek
East Providence, Rhode Island

Hook: Regular saltwater hook, sizes 1/0 to 4/0.
Thread: White 6/0.
Upper wing: White Ultra Hair, pearl Angel Hair, silver Angel Hair, chartreuse Angel Hair, and baitfish Angel Hair.
Lower wing: Pearl Angel Hair.
Eyes: Small chartreuse dome eyes.

Capt. Ray Stachelek spends all summer fishing for striped bass and bluefish, and he knows the value of durable, lifelike baitfish patterns. He fishes this silverside imitation with a stripping retrieve to mimic a fleeing baitfish. He prefers to use an intermediate or full-sinking line to keep the fly near the bottom.

Capt. Stachelek uses the newest synthetic materials to tie his baitfish patterns. These ingredients give the flies flash and durability.

Capt. Ray's Angel Hair Menhaden

tied by Capt. Ray Stachelek
East Providence, Rhode Island

Hook: Regular saltwater hook, sizes 1/0 to 4/0.
Thread: White 6/0.
Upper wing: White Ultra Hair, pearl gold Angel Hair, silver Angel Hair, pink Angel Hair, purple Angel Hair, and baitfish Angel Hair.
Lower wing: Pearl gold Angel Hair.
Eyes: Small silver dome eyes.

Menhaden are among the most important baitfish in the Northeast. If you're a seasoned saltwater fly rodder, you probably already have a selection of patterns to imitate this forage; if you're a new angler, you eventually will. Capt. Ray's Angel Hair Menhaden is a fly every Northeast fly fishermen will want to try. If you anticipate bumping into bluefish, be sure to use a length of wire tippet material; the sharp teeth of a bluefish will quickly slice regular leader material, and you'll loose this lovely fly.

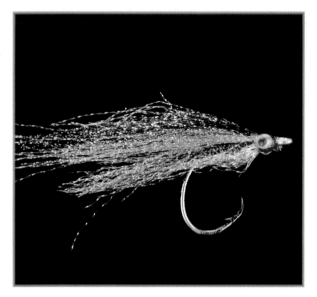

Albie Krystal Flash

tied by Capt. Randy Jacobson
Waterford, Connecticut

Hook: Eagle Claw 194C Circle Hook, size 2/0.
Thread: Red size A.
Body: Green sparkle braid.
Belly: Pearl Krystal Flash.
Wing: Pearl, gold and black Krystal Flash.
Eyes: Extra-small gold dome eyes.

Capt. Jacobson originally tied this pattern to catch false albacore, but soon learned that it would attract a wide variety of gamefish. Also, by substituting the colors of materials, it can be used as the basis for a wide variety of baitfish imitations.

Like with most baitfish patterns, use a stripping retrieve. Capt. Jacobson points out that since this fly is tied on a circle, be sure not to set the hook too quickly when the fish strikes; instead, when you feel the weight of the fish, just lift the rod and let the fish hook itself.

Grasshopper

tied by Capt. Richard Stuhr
Charleston, South Carolina

Hook: Regular saltwater hook, size 2.
Thread: Chartreuse 3/0.
Tail: Pearl Krystal Flash.
Body: Olive chenille.
Eyes: Small gold dumbbell or bead-chain.
Wing: Brown bucktail and grizzly hackle dyed brown.

"The grasshopper is a pattern I use mostly for tailing redfish in the spartina grass during the big full and new-moon tides from late spring through early fall," says Capt. Stuhr. "The reds are in the grass after the fiddler crabs, shrimp and anything else they come across. The grass is fairly thick and the red's vision cone seems to be pretty narrow. The idea is to get the fly in front of the fish without it fouling in the grass. I use the heavy eyes to sink the fly and to keep the hook point riding up. The chenille body gives the fly good bulk. The feathers give it life, and the Krystal Flash is a great eye-catcher.

"During the winter, we sight cast to reds in shallow water, and I have had great success fishing the Grasshopper with short strips."

Although the Grasshopper is not a lightweight—the eyes give the fly mass—it is comfortable to cast with a 7- or 8-weight rod, and a 9-foot-long, 12- to 16-pound-test leader.

VIP Popper

tied by Capt. Scott Sparrow
Rio Hondo/Arroyo City, Texas

Capt. Sparrow fishes the lower Laguna Madre area throughout the year for redfish and speckled trout. He fishes by boat, kayak and wading.

In describing the VIP Popper, Capt. Sparrow says, "The VIP Popper is a simple fly that possesses several qualities that are important when fishing clear, shallow water. Tied on a wide-gap, lightweight hook, the fly lands softly on the water, casts easily in the wind, makes a lot of noise when you need it to, and hooks fish reliably. It is made out of a block of closed-cell foam, slipped over the hook shank in front of a section of tail material and spun deer hair.

"After tying in the deer hair, wrap the thread forward and back to create a base for gluing the foam head to the hook shank. Use a bodkin needle to create a pilot hole through the bottom of the foam, and slip the foam onto the hook to check the fit. Remove the block of foam from the hook, smear epoxy on the thread wraps, and replace the foam head. Use doll eyes, rather than dome eyes, because the doll eyes add to the fly's buoyancy."

The VIP is a general attractor pattern. Capt. Sparrow recommends fishing it with short, steady strips for catching redfish; more erratic strips seem to attract the trout.

Hook: Gamakatsu B10S, size 6 or 4.
Thread: Size 3/0, your choice of color.
Tail: Strands of pink Flexi Floss, strands of pearl Flashabou, and deer hair.
Head: Closed-cell foam.
Eyes: Medium doll eyes epoxied to the head.
Weed guard: 20-pound-test monofilament.

Son of Clouser

tied by Capt. John Kumiski
Chuluota, Florida

Hook: Mustad 3407, sizes 4 to 1.
Thread: Black Flat Waxed Nylon.
Tail: Red squirrel tail hair.
Wing: Copper Flashabou and brown marabou.
Eyes: Small dumbbell eyes.
Head: Narrow brown chenille.

Here's another version of the ever-popular Clouser Minnow. Capt. Kumiski's version is excellent for catching redfish and several other species of fish that visit the flats. The marabou wing gives the fly a lot of motion when stripped through the water.

Capt. Kumiski fishes the Son of Clouser near the bottom with a slow, stripping retrieve. He fishes this fly with a variety of rod sizes depending upon the targeted species.

The Clouser Minnow is one of those patterns that is tied in almost every beginning fly-tying class. It's easy to tie and catches a huge variety of fish. Capt. Kumiski's Son of Clouser is a great variation.

Squirrel-Tail Clouser

tied by Capt. Richard Stuhr
Charleston, South Carolina

Hook: Regular saltwater hook, size 4.
Thread: Yellow 3/0.
Eye: Small brass dumbbell.
Tail: Tan Super Hair and copper Krystal Flash.
Wing: Red squirrel tail hair.

Capt. Stuhr uses this Bob Clouser-inspired pattern to catch redfish and bonefish. Capt. Stuhr says this is a good general imitation of a grass shrimp, and he fishes it in the spring with a slow, crawling retrieve; he tries to keep the fly near the bottom.

Mother's Day Fly #1

tied by Capt. Scott Sparrow
Rio Hondo/Arroyo City, Texas

Hook: Regular saltwater hook, sizes 6 and 4.
Thread: Black 6/0.
Tail: Pink marabou, pearl Flashabou, and brown saddle hackles.
Body: Pink Estaz and a ginger hackle spiral-wrapped over the body.
Feelers: Brown Flexi Floss.
Eyes: Pearl glass beads.

Capt. Sparrow uses his Mother's Day Fly any time of the day throughout the year. It is an impressionistic imitation of a shrimp, and catches speckled trout and redfish. Try this fly in shallow water, or tie it with heavier dumbbell eyes and fish it in deeper water.

Mother's Day Fly #2

tied by Capt. Scott Sparrow
Rio Hondo/Arroyo City, Texas

Hook: Regular saltwater hook, sizes 6 and 4.
Thread: Chartreuse 6/0.
Tail: Two strands of chartreuse Flexi Floss, a tuft of chartreuse marabou, and natural deer hair.
Eyes: Two chartreuse glass beads slipped onto a piece of 50-pound-test monofilament.
Body: Chartreuse Estaz.
Feelers: Two strands of chartreuse Flexi Floss.

Here's another of Capt. Sparrow's Mother's Day Flies. These patterns are fish-catching imitations of shrimp. Capt. Sparrow uses these flies to catch redfish and speckled trout. The Mother's Day Flies can be weighted to fish deep, but as shown here, they are light enough to fish with a 6-weight rod. In addition to catching the favorite gamefish around Laguna Madre, they will also catch bonefish and other flats species.

Hook: Regular saltwater hook, size 8.
Thread: Fine clear monofilament thread.
Underbody: Fine Mylar braid wrapped on
the hook shank.
Belly: Fine white craft fur.
Back: Fine olive craft fur.
Eyes: Small silver adhesive eyes.
Head: Epoxy.
Weed guard: 25-pound-test monofilament.

BP Special

tied by Capt. Tom McQuade
St. John, Virgin Islands

Capt. McQuade has a growing reputation for tying very inventive and realistic crab and crustacean imitations. You'll find several of these flies in my book, *Tying Contemporary Saltwater Flies*. I was especially pleased when he sent one of his baitfish patterns for this book.

The BP Special is very simple to tie. Begin by tying a length of fine, soft white craft fur to the hook. Tie on and wrap the tinsel underbody. Tie a narrow piece of olive craft fur on top of the body to create the back of the fly, and tie on the looped weed guard. Place a small adhesive eye on each side of the body, mix a batch of five-minute epoxy, and coat the head. As the epoxy begins to stiffen, lightly pull back the craft fur to create a narrow, streamlined head. Note that Capt. McQuade clips the white craft fur at an angle to create a belly on the fly.

The BP Special imitates a variety of small Caribbean baitfish, but will be at home in the Northeast and many other waters. This is a lightweight pattern, perfect for casting with a 6- or 7-weight rod. Fish the BP Special at various depths with short strips.

Polar Mile

tied by Garret Booth
Temple, New Hampshire

This fly has proven successful at all times of the year and at all times of the day," says Garret Booth. "Our preference for fishing times usually tends to be during calm weather conditions. The farther down the water column we fish, the larger the patterns we will use. We fish the smaller sizes up on the flats, but in deeper water we go much larger—patterns up to size 4/0.

"I like to go large since some of the striped bass we connect with are of 'decent' health and size. I fish a ten-weight rod, and love an intermediate-sinking line. When fishing the larger patterns—at the mouth of the Merrimack River, for example—I like to send this fly down with a Teeny three-hundred-fifty-grain line and fish it slowly. Strip retrieve this fly to keep it moving and the tail undulating. The main goal is to get the Krystal Flash moving, and the polar-bear hair enhances the flash

"As far as the saltwater species go, Cape Ann has an incredible number of opportunities for shore and boat anglers alike. The Merrimack River is within most people's reach here in New Hampshire, whether they fish by boat or wading. The Parker River and Joppa Flats offer great chances at substantial fish due to their accessibility and quieter water."

Hook: Tiemco TMC800S, sizes 4 to 4/0.
Thread: Danville 210, white.
Tail: Polar bear hair topped with white FisHair and five strands of pearl Krystal Flash.
Body: Pearl Mylar tinsel.
Wing: White, pink, and purple bucktail.
Topping: Peacock herl.
Throat: Red calftail.
Eyes: Small silver dome eyes, coated with epoxy.

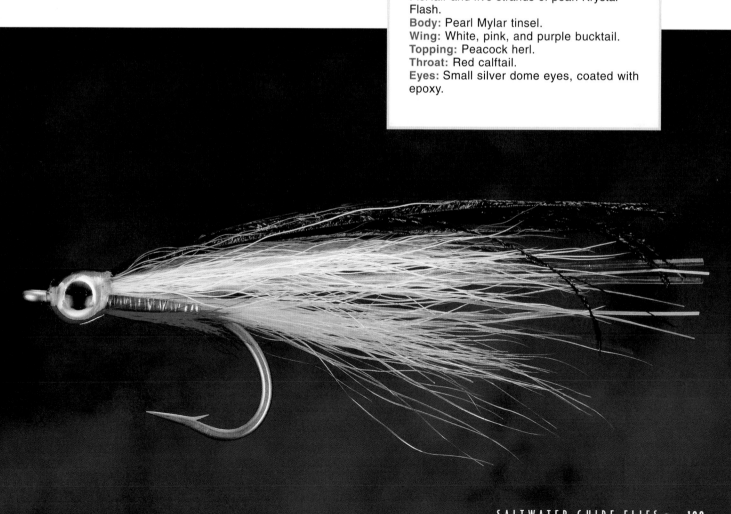

Floating Spotted Blue-tipped Crab

tied by Capt. Tom McQuade
St. John, Virgin Islands

Hook: Regular saltwater hook, size 4.
Thread: Fine clear monofilament thread.
Eyes: Melted monofilament.
Body: Grizzly hackle, wrapped up the hook shank and clipped to shape.
Legs and claws: Grizzly hackle. Color the tips of the claws with a blue permanent marker.
Back: Heavy sheet plastic or a small piece cut from a plastic beverage container.
Weed guard: 30-pound-test monofilament.

Most of Capt. Tom McQuade's crab patterns are designed to fish close to the bottom; this is the first of his floating crab imitations that I have seen. Capt. McQuade specializes in fishing the Virgin Islands's marl flats for bonefish, and this is fast becoming one of his favorite flies for catching those prized fish.

The back of the Floating Spotted Blue-tipped Crab is very interesting.

Monkey Brain

tied by Garret Booth
Temple, New Hampshire

Hook: Gamakatsu Octopus, sizes 1/0 and 2/0.
Thread: Danville 210, white.
Tail: Four white saddle hackles.
Hackle collar: White, highlighted with pearl Krystal Flash.
Body: Pearl Mylar tinsel.
Eyes: Medium silver dome eyes coated with epoxy.

This fly has proven successful at all times of the year and at all times of the day," says Garret Booth. "Our preference is to fish first light and when the water is very calm. So far, we fish Money Brains as an attractor, but it also imitates the fluttering fall of a stunned or wounded baitfish.

"For stripers, we fish this pattern up tight against the cut banks that occur on many tidal rivers. The majority of the fish caught on this fly take it 'on the fall.' Fish it close to the bank, near bridge abutments, or any structure, for that matter.

"This fly flutters as it falls to the water, driving the albies and bonito crazy. It's small enough so as not to turn them off, with enough finesse to create a little curiosity. It's not too heavy, so it tends to stay in the upper reaches of the water column, which is the key ingredient to hooking up with these fish. Strip retrieve the fly to get it back to the top of the water column, then let it fall again.

"In all conditions, we fish this fly with an intermediate-sinking line to allow for maximum diversity."

The Whistlin' Mac

tied by Mac McGee
Chattanooga, Tennessee

Hook: Regular saltwater hook, sizes 1/0 to 3/0.
Thread: Black 3/0.
Tail: Chartreuse Zonker strip, strands of silver holographic tinsel for a wing, and white bucktail on the top, bottom, and sides. Tie a grizzly hackle on each side of the Zonker strip.
Hackle: Grizzly saddle hackle.
Eyes: Silver bead chain.
Head: Chartreuse Crystal Chenille.

The Whistlin' Mac catches tarpon, redfish and snook, as well as largemouth and smallmouth bass. It's a variation of Dan Blanton's Whistler, a very popular saltwater pattern. Mac's Whistler, just like Blanton's Whistler, is a general baitfish imitation. Fish these flies with a jigging and stripping retrieve.

Green Molly

tied by Capt. Jeff Northrop
Westport, Connecticut

Hook: Tiemco TMC800S, size 1/0.
Thread: Clear monofilament.
Tail: Green saddle hackles.
Body: Green deer hair.
Eyes: Doll eyes.

This is a great slow-water fly with lots of life," Capt. Northrop says. "Fish it with a floating or intermediate-sinking line. Use a stripping retrieve, and let it pause between strips. It's deadly!"

In addition to guiding, Capt. Northrop is also an FFF certified casting instructor. He has taught the likes of Martha Stewart and Paul Newman the finer points of casting.

Hook: Mustad 34184 jig hook, size 1.
Thread: White 6/0.
Head: Large gold cone.
Body: Small pearl EZ Body tubing.

Sparkle Plenty

tied by Capt. Larry Kennedy
St. Simons Island, Georgia

Capt. Kennedy's Sparkle Plenty is designed for catching tarpon, shark, ladyfish, redfish, and sea trout. It requires only a couple of ingredients and is easy to tie.

The Mustad 34184 is a very interesting hook. Note that the shank is bent at about a 45-degree angle. This hook is perfect for tying flies that will fish with a jigging action and that are almost snagproof.

Bozo Bunker

tied by Capt. Jeff Northrop
Westport, Connecticut

Capt. Jeff Northrop has been a key player in popularizing saltwater fly fishing in the Northeast. Jerry Gibbs, the fishing editor for *Outdoor Life* magazine, says that Jeff is credited with introducing "flats style fly fishing and flats boats, and is the primary catalyst in firing the recent excitement in saltwater fly fishing in these latitudes." That's very high praise, indeed.

Capt. Jeff spends most of his time fishing the Norwalk Islands located off Westport and Norwalk, Connecticut. These are the islands where Ernest Hemingway and Michael Lerner, the force behind the foundation of the International Game Fish Association, set the early records for catching stripped bass with flies. These islands are known for having huge stripped bass, as well as record bluefish and false albacore.

According to Jeff, "the reasons the islands have produced so many record fish over the years is directly tied to their location on the migratory path of the Hudson River stripers. The vast herds of fish leave the Hudson in late April and May, and journey north in search of abundant food sources. The Norwalk Islands, which are located fifty-two miles from the mouth of the Hudson and directly at the mouths of seven rivers and streams, provide a virtual supermarket for these migrating fish."

The Bozo Bunker is typical of the types of flies Capt. Northrop is using to catch the big striped bass around the Norwalk Islands. Bozo Hair is a favorite material of fly tiers who dress large saltwater baitfish patterns. Originally used for making clown wigs, it is now available in many fly shops, especially in the Northeast. The material is tough, absorbs no water, and comes in many colors. While used to imitate menhaden, you can tie the Bozo Bunker in a variety of sizes and colors to imitate many baitfish.

Hook: Tiemco TMC600SP, size 2/0.
Thread: Gray Monocord.
Tail: Pink Flashabou and Bozo Hair.
Body: White Bozo Hair.
Back: Blue or green Bozo Hair
Throat: Red Krystal Flash.
Eyes: Doll eyes.

Hook: Gamakatsu SC-15, sizes 2 to 5/0.
Thread: White Flat Waxed Nylon (you may substitute with your choice of color).
Body: Sexy Fibre in you choice of colors (a material such as Bozo Hair is a good substitute), and strands of Fly Flash material.
Eyes: Large silver dome eyes.

Sexy Fly Slender Minnow

tied by Capt. John Kumiski
Chuluota, Florida

Capt. John Kumiski has been fly fishing for forty years and guiding for the past fifteen. Capt. Kumiski offers a variety of fishing options—skiff, kayak, canoe, and wading—but all involve sight-fishing. He leads his clients to Florida's redfish, sea trout, snook, tarpon, and black drum. Capt. Kumiski specializes in fishing Indian River Lagoon, Banana River Lagoon, and Mosquito Lagoon. He also fishes the beaches between Boca Grande and Sanibel for tarpon.

The Sexy Slender Fly Minnow is a good general baitfish imitation. Capt. Kumiski uses a material called Sexy Fibre to tie the body, but many crinkly synthetic hairs will work. Tie a bunch of fibers at the end of the hook shank; the fibers should extend back about three to four times the length of the shank, and extend forward about two to three times the length of the shank. Bend the forward fibers back over the top and tie down. Advance the thread forward, and add more bunches of fibers. Be sure to add a bunch to the bottom of the shank to form the belly of the fly. Mix colors to create a natural mottled affect. Epoxy a dome eye onto each side of the head.

The synthetic fibers are very durable, and a well-tied Sexy Fly Slender Minnow will survive fights with many fish. Capt. Kumiski fishes this pattern with a 6- to 12-weight outfit, depending upon the targeted species. He usually uses leaders between 9 to 14 feet long, and between 12 and 14 pounds test. Leader selection depends upon the clarity of the water and the targeted species.

APPENDIX: GOOD GUIDES

Baltz, Thomas
328 Zion Road
Mt. Holly Springs, Pennsylvania 17065
717-486-7438
baltzte@aol.com

Bauer, Peter J.
Anglers Edge
1420 A, Highway 395
(775) 782-4734
Gardnerville, Nevada
anglersedge@ableweb.net

Bastian, Don
Don Bastian's Angling Specialties
1740 St. Michaels Road
Cogan Station, Pennsylvania 17728
(570) 998-2481

Berg, Ed
1028 Via La Paz
San Pedro, California 90732
310-547-2444
edflyfisher@aol.com

Betters, Fran
Fran Better's Adirondack Sport Shop
P.O. Box 125
Wilmington, New York 12997
518-946-2605
adirondackflyfishing.com

Booth, Garret
Grey's Angling
98 Webster Highway
Temple, New Hampshire 03084
(603) 924-2396
albienut@prodigy.net

Buchner, Jay
Buchner Fly Designs
P.O. Box 1022
Jackson, Wyoming 83001
307-733-4944
jbuchner@wyoming.net

Burkholder, Ken
1212 Shoshone Street
Boise, Idaho 83705
208-331-3474
kenburk@rmci.net

Cameron, Ian
Penobscot Drift Boats
354 Holden Road
Glenburn, Maine 04401-1201
207-942-2522
ripgorge@hotmail.com
www.rivertherapy.com

Chipman, Reg "Chip"
P.O. Box 274
Nutrioso, Arizona 85932
928-339-4829
chip@cybertrails.com
www.azmtflyfishing.com

Cowen, Henry
Cowen's Quality Flies & Guide Service
3510 Lake Breeze Lane
Gainesville, Florida 30506
678-450-1133
henryc@evy.com

Duran, Deborah
Bear's Den Fly Fishing Shop
98 Summer Street
Taunton, Massachusetts 02780
508-880-6226
beardenfly@aol.com
www.bearsden.cc

Ehlers, Capt. Pat
The Fly Fishers
9617 W. Greenfield Ave.
Milwaukee, Wisconsin 53214
414-259-8100
theflyfishers1@aol.com
www.theflyfishers.com

Fink, Tom
The Sporting Gentleman
306 E. Baltimore Pike
Media, Pennsylvania 19063
610-565-6140
www.sportinggentleman.com

Furimsky, Ben
P.O. Box 2986
Crested Butte, Colorado
970-349-2752
highpeak@crestedbutte.net

Gibbens, Capt. Kent
Backcountry Charter Service
270 Greenwood Circle
Ormond Beach, Florida 31274
386-672-8929
kentgibbens@aol.com
backcountrycaptain.com

Huff, Mac
P.O. Box 865
Joseph, Oregon 97846
800-940-3688
machuff@oregontrail.net

Jacobson, Capt. Randy
Release One Charters
16 Bishop Street
Waterford, Connecticutt 06385
860 437 9768
releaseone@swnet.net
saltwaterflies.com/link

Jordan, Gloria
Gloria Jordan's Fly Rod Shop
P.O. Box 667, Route 7A
Manchester Center, Vermont 05255
802-362-3186

Kashner, Chuck
P.O. Box 127
Pawlet, Vermont 05761
1-800-682-0103
ckashner@msn.com
www.chuckkashner.com

Keller, Capt. Al
810 12th Ave. South
Naples, Florida 34102
239-564-4711
fishalkeller@earthlink.net

Kennedy, Capt. Larry
3405 Frederica Road
St. Simons Island, Georgia 31522
912-638-5454
www.stsimonsoutfitters.com

Kozlowski, Ron
RR 1, Box 1092
Nicholson, Pennsylvania 18446
570-942-6333
ronsflies@aol.com

Kumiski, Capt. John
284 Clearview Road
Chuluota, Florida 32766
407-977-5207
spottedtail@spottedtail.com
www.spottedtail.com

Kuss, Mary
The Sporting Gentleman
306 E. Baltimore Pike
Media, Pennsylvania 19063
610-565-6140
www.sportinggentleman.com

Legere, Dan
Maine Guide Fly Shop & Guide Service
34 Moosehead Lake Road
Greenville, Maine 04441
207-695-2266
flyshop@moosehead.net
www.maineguideflyshop.com

Lewis, Robert
16 Dogwood Hills
Pound Ridge, New York 10576
914-764-1393

McGee, Mac
Choo Choo Fly & Tackle
40 Frazier Ave.
Chattanooga, Tennessee 37405
423-267-0024
www.choochoofly.com

McLean, Rob
Freestone Flies & Guide Service
2145 Los Altos Drive
Rawlins, Wyoming 82301
307-324-2014
quillbod@coffey.com
www.freestoneflies.us

McQuade, Tom
P.O. Box 161
St. John, U.S. Virgin Islands
340-693-9446
tommcquade@att.net

Mallard, Bob
Kennebec River Outfitters
469 Lakewood Road
Madison, Maine 04590
207-474-2500
www.kennebecriveroutfitters.com

Mastaler, Tony
13 Downer Hill
Springfield, Vermont 05156
802-885-2084

Moeykens, Justin
Hunter's Angling Supplies
Central Square
New Boston, New Hampshire 03070
603-487-3388
Trouthunter@email.com

Murphy, Rick
Angler's Covey
917 W. Colorado Ave.
Colorado Springs, Colorado 80905
719-471-2984
rphlyphish@cs.com

Murray, Harry
Murray's Fly Shop
P.O. Box 156
Edinburgh, Virginia 22824
540-984-4212
www.murraysflyshop.com

Northrop, Capt. Jeff
Westport Outfitters
570 Riverside Ave.
Westport, Connecticut 06880
203-226-1915
www.saltwater-flyfishing.com

Paulson, Matt
The Superior Fly Angler
310 Belknap
Superior, Wisconsin 54880
715-395-9520
flyshop@cpinternet.com
www.superiorflyangler.com

Pecci, Capt. Dave
Obsession Sportfishing Charters
144 Whiskeag Road
Bath, Maine 04530
207-442-8581
dave@obsessioncharters.com
www.obsessioncharters.com

Polacek, Todd
Madison Outfitters, Ltd.
7475 Mineral Point Road
Madison, Wisconsin 53717
608-833-1359
madout@chorus.net

Savard, Tim & Lisa
Lopstick Outfitters
First Connecticut Lake
Pittsburgh, New Hampshire 03592
1-800-538-6659
www.lopstick.com

Sickau, Scott
Hatch's Fly Tying Supplies
503 W. 7th
Boone, Iowa 50036-2523
515-432-6026
hatch@willinet.net

Sparrow, Capt. Scott
Kingfisher Inn & Guide Service
36901 Marshall Hutts Road
Rio Hondo/Arroyo City, Texas 78583
956-748-4350
kingfisher@lagunamadre.net
www.lagunamadre.net

Staats, Barry
The Sporting Gentleman
306 E. Baltimore Pike
Media, Pennsylvania 19063
610-565-6140
www.sportinggentleman.com

Stachelek, Capt. Ray
Cast a Fly Charters
21 Plymouth Road
East Providence, Rhode Island 02914
401-434-6660
castaflycharters@cs.com
www.castaflycharters.com

Stahl, William
Bunkhouse Lodge
Everest Street
P.O. Box 377
Wilmington, NY 12997
518-946-2602
adkbunkhouse@yahoo.com
www.bunkhouse.com

Stuhr, Capt. Richard
547 Sanders Farm Lane
Charleston, South Carolina 29492
843-881-3179
captstuhr@msn.com
www.captstuhr.com

Turck, Guy
High Country Flies
P.O. Box 3432
185 N. Center St.
Jackson, Wyoming 83001
307-733-7210
info@highcountryflies.com
www.turcktarantula.com

Wagner, Capt. Scott
3311 Bannon Drive
Thunderbolt, Georgia 31404
912-308-3700
www.savannahfly.com

Wissmath, Dusty
Dusty Wissmath's Fly Fishing School
and Guide Service
18116 Raven Rocks Road
Bluemont, Virginia 20135
540-554-2676
www.dwflyfishingschool.com

Youngers, Rich
Creekside Fly Fishing
345 High Street SE
Salem, Oregon 97301
(503) 588-1768
www.creeksideflyfishing.com

INDEX OF FLIES AND GUIDES